Everything Leading to the First English

Alasdair Gray

Mr MacQuedy (producing a large scroll): "In the infancy of society . . ."
The Rev Dr Folliott: Pray, Mr Macquedy, how is it that all gentlemen of your nation begin everything they write with the "infancy of society"?
(*Crotchet Castle* by Thomas Love Peacock)

Babies embarrass masterful men, who find it queer that once they too could only wail, suck and excrete. When one year old we totter through a belwildering world on unsteady legs while small birds of the same age have already flown, mated, built nests and begun feeding their own children. What unique ability develops in the following years which enables us to handle the world in so many surprising ways? Some say nothing but the strength and intelligence to grab what we want, even from our own kind, and do it in gangs. We would have nothing worth grabbing if that were the whole truth. Our unique ability is to imagine and make something new which can be shared with others. Conversation, not theft, most explains us. It supplies and shapes the whole matter of our thought, yet we think little of it because all vocal creatures use it. Birds start singing before dawn to stir each other into briskness for the day ahead, then keep up a quieter texture of noise till sunset, announcing their position and territory with calls which also tell when they are congregating toward food or dispersing from a danger. Cats meowl in chorus to declare their separate identities, sexual readiness, and united cattishness. For the same reasons our ancestors the tree-rodents probably scolded and chattered a lot.

Though bigger than squirrels they were as alert, inquisitive, and varied in their diet, eating nuts, snails, berries, eggs, carrion, fruit and lice. Conscious choice (*dare I eat a peach? Shall I part my hair behind?*) began with this variety of edibles and increased when we came to scramble on the ground. Like pigs we grubbed up roots, like foxes grabbed fresh meat, but we grubbed and grabbed with our forepaws, not snouts and teeth. Our faces were free to play with a range of utterances and expressions which should still be one of our great freedoms. Some scientists think the big human brain developed through ape people discovering more and more things to do with their hands while using these to do more and more things. Our ability to remember and choose between a large number of actions at last wiped from our nerves all but one inbred skill other beasts use, replacing the rest by a wholly new one.

The surviving instinct is imitation; the new one is making shareable signs for things. Both appear in children learning to talk. They get words by imitating their elders, while inventing names of their own for their favourite objects. The inventions are usually ignored, and even if not the children stop using them because imitated words are more useful, but this private gibberish shows intelligence, not folly. At the same age children without dolls take a handy object and treat it as they want to be treated or as they wish to treat others. They make it a sign of life and hold communion with it. By shaping sounds and handling objects, by attaching memories and hopes to them we learn to converse with ourselves and others. Conversing with ourselves is thinking. Conversation with others enlarges that.

About 6000 centuries ago folk like us began moving through the world, each generation surviving by habits learned from elders but habits which could change in a lifetime if the surroundings changed. From a genesis in Africa our tribes moved to Asia, peopling the Chinese plains so densely that most big migrations after that pushed west and south, though ten thousand years before Christ some Asian families crossed the Bering strait into America and began peopling it from the north-east. "Men can get used to anything. What scoundrels they are!" said Dostoevski, recalling life in a Russian prison camp. In a half million years our tiny tribes went everywhere, sometimes fighting each other for fruitful territories but usually adapting to a world they could not change much. It passed through three ice ages. where food was abundant our average height became six feet or more. Usually we were more dwarfish because we kept exhausting food supplies or becoming too many for them. Our skins grew pale in the cloudy north, black in the equatorial south and in east Asia lost a fold of eyelid, but our racial differences were slight because everywhere we strove to keep the same pattern of brain and skeleton by changing our minds, tools, clothes and houses. We changed them through conversation, invention and imitation, being all the time goaded by questions no human brain can avoid.

How did I get here?

What must I do to live?

Where in the world am I going?

These are the first questions children brood upon when they start thinking. Answering them created the vocabulary, art, science and faith of early as well as modern people.

Early answers have been deduced by seeing how the earliest known stories of the pastoral Egyptians and Greeks agree with those of tribes still living in prehistoric ways. Most folk who live directly from the earth believe all they see and feel is alive and holy, and all earthly creatures were originally born by earth through a sexual wedding with the sky. They believe death will return them to a timeless state already occupied by ancestors who converse with them through traditions, memories and dreams. They do not think themselves more important to the world than the flocks or kangaroos they depend on or the crocodiles they dread. Their customs and taboos are intended to revive the beasts and ground that feeds them. Most tribes have a priest-doctor to ease pains and illness with traditional prayers and remedies, who recites the stories of the tribal ancestors, and is sometimes inspired by a crisis to say what they would have done. Many bushmen and esquimaux are so widely scattered that they do without governments. Closer-knit tribes are co-ordinated through assemblies of family heads, one of whom judges disputes between them and speaks for them in dealings with other tribes. A younger member of the leader's family sometimes inherits the job, but if incompetent gets replaced by someone the assembly prefers.

Fewer folk got born before the first city was built than were born in the first sixty years of the twentieth century. They discovered all the main skills we now live by, the skills which make our science possible. The cleverest modern invention is a self-firing bullet which carried three men to the moon and back, burning most of itself up on the way. Imagined beside the first efficient axe, canoe or plough it seems astonishingly useless. Yet we can feel why most in the 19th century who first glimpsed how long people had lived on earth had a low opinion of the first human tribes, believing they were practically speechless or had nothing very good to say because they lived without writing. City dwellers also want simple answers to the question, "How did I get here?" and who can start trying to imagine over half a million years of human life - at least 240,000 nameless generations - without weariness and despair? It is a surer reminder of death and the end of fame than a tour of all France's military graveyards. So we call the first ninety-nine percent of human history *prehistory*: a hardly readable preface to a tale which starts a few centuries before Moses and Homer, takes in all the great human names and leads straight to you and me.

Settled farming began. In fertile places folk grew so productive and thick on the ground that they supported market places where craftsmen dealt in woven goods, pottery and metal utensils. I like to imagine these places expanding through peaceful trade into the earliest cities. Plato thought the first city-states were made by armed hunters on horseback invading valleys of farming people and building central strongholds from which to plunder them. Both things happened.

Between six and four thousand years ago twenty cities of at least 10,000 people were built in Asia and north-west Africa, each for a while the capital of a nation formed and destroyed and reformed by combinations of trade and conquest. They were as different from each other as modern Peking, Delhi, Rome, New York etc, but had some things in common. Each stood on a plain beside a great river, among fertile farms productive of grain. At harvest time the city revenue officers, who were priests aided by soldiers or vice versa, gathered much of the grain inside the city walls where it became the wealth of the state: the food of folk who did not live by producing what was essential to life but by managing those who did. A big grain store had the power of a modern bank; those who owned it had time to consider problems of survival from a leisurely distance. A sack of grain could nourish a family for a fortnight, so might be used to buy both goods and labour, and buy them cheap in years of famine. Beside a priesthood, army and craftsmen each city had a class of slaves originally created through warfare; but later people - even the original producers of the grain - sometimes sold themselves into slavery to avoid starvation. And each city had a king, originally the commander of a conquering army. Such armies only work with a supreme commander, and when successful can put him in charge of everything. Since underlings grow uncontrollable in states where the bosses openly fight each other for power, the officers of state supported a single boss who in peacetime inherited the job from his dad. This stabilised ruling classes but ensured that a good king was a lucky accident, or that anyone could do the job. It was too shameful an arrangement to be openly admitted. Kins were advertised as deputies and descendants of a great god in the sky - the sun itself - and most of them believed it.

When social grabbing and shoving dominating architecture it builds

Norman castles, Victorian prisons and cotton mills, modern tower blocks, car parks and shopping centres: structures designed to take in as much as possible at a few guarded entrances and elsewhere show nothing but forbidding surfaces. Most cities have looked better than that. Borges describes how one appeared to a barbarian it attracted.

> He sees something he has never seen, or has not seen . . . in such plenitude. He sees the day and cypresses and marble. He sees a whole that is complex and yet without disorder; he sees a city, an organism composed of statues, temples, gardens, dwellings, stairways, urns, capitals, of regular and open spaces. None of these artifacts impresses him (I know) as beautiful; they move him as we might be moved today by a complex machine of whose purpose we are ignorant but in whose design we intuit an immortal intelligence.

The intelligence which makes a city attractive is knowledge and craftsmanship working for the good of the majority; in the variety of convenient goods and luxuries which are suggested, made and shared when many sorts of people talk together. But knowledge dies if not widely shared. Some cities had libraries of law tables, religious and medical treatises, historical and astronomical records, maps, poems, stories and tax registers: all destroyed when the small class who used them was defeated by conquerors of a different tongue. The Aryans who destroyed the earliest Indian cities and their writings did without writing for a thousand years. All the writings of ancient Babylon, Crete, Carthage and Etruria have vanished except a few indecipherable inscriptions. Many Egyptian and Assyrian texts survived but for fifteen centuries nobody could read them. Only China was so densely peopled and efficiently organised that every conqueror before the Euro-American invasion of 1839 had to govern it by learning the ways, language and the writing of the conquered.

But the learning in the shattered libraries was not wholly lost. Every alphabet the world uses was adapted from the scripts of Sumeria, Assyria and Egypt by nomads and seafarers who traded with them. These mobile people needed letters for contracts and bills. They also wrote large agreements which are the best human laws, with some undiscussable dictates which are the worst. Then they wrote down the best songs and accounts of the heroes who made their nations, and so many loved these books that buildings were not needed to preserve them, the national epics were so continually copied and recited. Ancestors of literate folk started talking to them through books. Imaginative descendants talked back. The book of Isiah was put beside Moses, the plays of Aristophanes beside Homer, so later readers heard their ancestors talking to each other. Different national literatures began conversing. Oriental Buddhism happened when some Indian texts reached scholars in China, inspiring them with hunger for more. Barriers of desert and perplexingly different script stopped Indian and Chinese books informing European readers, but the thought of half the world has been shaped by intercourse *between*, intercourse *with* the books of three Mediterranean nations.

The earliest and most influential books belonged to the nation which commanded the least territory and sometimes none. They have lasted over

3000 years because they were the shared intellectual homeland of people who sometimes had no other. The Jews were wandering herdsmen who became guest workers in Egypt, first in a privileged state, then, as their numbers increased, in an oppressed one. They got so used to settled life in Egypt that when their slavery grew unbearable they escaped to the desert intending to make a homeland in Canaan, but a generation passed before they were strong enough for invasion and conquest. In the years between escaping political oppression and founding their state by more of it they put in writing a queer and powerful idea: the world and its creatures were not originally born from acts of love but acts of will expressed through language. One eternally single masterful man-god imagined light, sky, sea, sun, moon, dry land, the plants and creatures, then made them in that order by naming them. This took five days. On the sixth he made a man out of earth to be the owner of the earth, and made him of a mature age because nobody can manage a big property when young and babies embarrass masterful men. From one of the earth man's spare ribs god made him a wife, to reproduce copies of him by the animal method. But Adam lost his great property by obeying his wife instead of the god who made him. He and his descendants became miserable toilers and wanderers to the time they escaped from Egypt, when the one god offered the Jews a special contract: if they would follow and have faith in nothing but his words he would give them a secure homeland.

This creation story insults women and defies every commonsense fact except one: where people and nations constantly jostle each other for territory nobody feels secure, and many think life is a crisis between a once happier state and a future they hope will be happier for their childen at least. Moses told a horde of fleeing gypsies that they were potential landlords, that the world had been made for them by an imagination and will like their own, and could be repossessed. In a century the Israelites made the contract he had drawn up with god on Ben Sinai come true. They were inspired to grab a land of milk, vines and cities from the Philistines, a race of sea-raiders who had grabbed it a century or two earlier. Many folk wanted that land. In the eight centuries before Jesus the Jews were conquered by the empires of Assyria, Babylon, Persia, Greece and Rome, disasters which they read as punishment for ignoring God's word or as tests of their faith in it. Later the Eden-to-Canaan story became the first gospel of the Christians and Mohammedans because it explained their feeling that life was a crisis too. It could also be twisted to justify almost any war. Arabs, Crusaders, Spaniards, British, Americans and Israelis have soothed their consciences with it while killing and robbing weaker people. But the Hebrew bible is not a safe prop for heads of state unless they have popular support. God in these books is not symbolised as a man in a strong position. The Jews thought it blasphemy to symbolise him at all. God is the creating mind known by the truth of words spoken through the mouth of anyone: a preacher denouncing those who cheat the poor of their property and try to bribe god with religious services, a survivor lamenting among the ruins of a city, an outcast crying in the wilderness. The Hebrew gospels contain good songs, stories and sermons which don't mention god at all. Many kinds of education can be got from it.

There is a different account of Mediterranean life in the poems of Homer, which tell how a lot of small piratical Greek states and islands combined to attack the city of Troy, and the adventures of one pirate on his way home. The Greeks were descended from Eurasian invaders who learned from Egyptian, Jewish and Carthaginian traders. Their ships and manners resembled those of the Vikings, their communities were not much more than a chieftain's palace with some adjacent farmsteads and a harbour, yet Homer's poems have almost universal human sympathy. The besieged Trojans are presented as more noble than the invading Greeks, nor is the Greek victory a success story. All leaders in that war are shown as eventually losing life, dignity and decency by it, while periodically discussing with a sort of baffled wonder the insufficient reasons for fighting like this in the first place. They talk like intelligent soldiers in any war. Yet along with the wasteful fights, strategies and excursions Homer describes the work by which life is maintained: how cattle are slaughtered and cooked, how a household launders its sheets, the design of a woman's woolwork basket and the pruning of a hedge. When a hero and his men get trapped in a cave by a one-eyed giant, half the story is how the monster keeps his flock of sheep, makes cheese of their milk and loves a favourite ram. Homer's view of life is tragic. He has no hope that human history will ever make up for the unjust things people do to each other, but mingled in the tragedy he shows the eternal gods who are the cause of it and comic relief from it. The Greek gods are man-like and woman-like too. They are the undying forms of love, wisdom, belligerence, art, craft and government which inspire us to greatness yet turns us against each other.

By the fifth century before Christ there were many literate Greek states and colonies round the Mediterranean and some developed conversation to an astonishing extent. in Athens every man who was not a slave or immigrant was expected to attend parliament and openly discuss matters which in other cities led to riots and bloodshed. Should Athens go to war or make peace? Should workmen be compensated for injury by their employer or by the state? Could local millionaires justify their huge incomes? Was the price of food to high? Decisions on these matters were reached by a majority vote and the defeated minority accepted the decisions as law until they could get them reversed. In the city square public lectures and discussions were a common source of entertainment. Is the best system of government monarchy, aristocracy or democracy? What makes a man a good citizen? Is the sun a white-hot ball of iron larger than the Greek mainland or a whirlpool of fiery particles which coalesce on the horizon with the dawn? Is the universe made by chance operating on a chaos of elements with eternity to play about in, or did an eternal mind form it from the start? And how do the other people answer these questions? For though the Athenians thought themselves special they knew that the customs which made them special had been picked up from other people or recently invented.

This Athenian freedom of thought, speech and action was financed by a naval fund. Other Greek states paid Athens to protect them from the vast empire of Persia in the east, and if they refused to pay the Athenian navy attacked them. Over the bodies of men killed in that warfare an Athenian statesman announced that Athens was setting the world such great examples of democratic tolerance, social welfare and civic achievement that the

Illustration by Alasdair Gray,
from *Unlikely Stories Mostly* (Canongate, 1983)

neighbours should gladly pay for these; but they didn't. The Athenians left great writing: among it the history of how their empire was destroyed by the wars to maintain it.

Only the Romans ruled for centuries over many other lands. Rome began as a small republic of belligerent farmers. Theirs was not a democracy on the Athenian plan. the plebeians were represented in the senate by just enough elected speakers to give the state unity in a crisis. Rich families managed the government and officered the army, writing their laws and reports in clear, curt, pithy Latin. Using Latin they conquered and taxed every civilisation round the Mediterranean and many tribal nations beyond, but Romans who wanted ideas along with big estates stocked their libraries with Greek writing. For centuries Greek poetry, history and philosophy were as beyond the scope of a Latin author as the Greek art of making bronze statues was beyond the Roman craftsmen. As the republic ended in conspiracies and civil war some Romans feared their achievement and language was also ending. The best account of Mediterranean civilisation was still Homer's. If Rome ended without getting into a great book then the best thing its empire had done was preserve and propagate the work of the Greeks.

Twenty-seven years before Christ, Augustus Caesar became first Roman emperor with the help of Maecenas, the richest and cleverest Roman banker. After defeating all his rivals in the civil war Augustus (I quote the Oxford Classical Dictionary) "assured freedom of trade and wealth to the upper classes," and, "gave peace, as long as it was consistent with the interests of the empire and the myth of his glory." He and Maecenas knew a Latin poet who cared for human culture and had proved it by writing fine poems about the cultivation of land, doing for Italy what the Greek poets Hesiod and Theocritus had done: make verse about peaceful farming and everyday faith. Encouraged and funded by the most powerful men in the new empire, Virgil, who hated war, wrote a Roman epic to rival Homer and justify the Roman conquests.

He had no crude love of earthly power, and like all deep thinkers on human history was more disturbed by the sufferings of the defeated than dazzled by splendid winners. He did not describe the empire growing from a small thatched republican town to a marble-surfaced, world-bullying capital. His story describes the struggles of a Trojan refugee, Aeneas, who escapes from Troy while the Greeks loot and burn it. Aeneas leads his son and a few survivors round several Mediterranean shores, suffering hardship and abandoning the woman he loves before reaching Italy and fighting to found the state which will become Rome. Homer's heroes (Achilles and Ulysses) are moved by a greed for fame, wealth and luxuries. Virgil's Aeneas is a modest, careful, steady man guided like Moses by one idea: to get a home for his people. During his struggle the gods encourage him with a vision of the future when his greatest descendant, Augustus Caesar, will make a peaceful home for all mankind by becoming the first emperor to rule Europe, Asia and Africa. Virgil fell ill before completing the epic and died after ordering his secretaries to burn it. He has been called a perfectionist who did not want to be remembered by something incomplete. The obvious reason is his loss of faith in government by conquest, loss of faith in Caesarism. Augustus Caesar preserved and published the Aeneid. It has been used to excuse him and his kind ever since. Kaisers and Czars adopted his family name. Dutch, English, French and German kings have been sculptured in the armour his statues wear. Most autocrats prefer imitation to creation.

In his novel *The Confidence Man* Herman Melville says few books contain a truly original character and no book can contain more than one. A truly original character (says Melville) makes the readers see themselves in a wholly new way, and he mentions Hamlet and Milton's Lucifer. He had Jesus of Nazareth in mind but was too cunning to say so. All we know of Jesus is four short books written in a Jewish dialect over fifty years after his crucifixion. They describe him as the living body of the god who made the universe and say he loved and loves people equally, even his enemies. They say he will give eternal life and happiness to all who believe in him, and prove it by loving each other and forgiving who hurt them. This message is either total rubbish or tells the whole truth about how we should live with each other. Hardly anyone has the strength to wholly accept or reject it, and those who explain why they partly reject and partly accept it end by describing themselves. The portrait is never flattering. I am introducing elements of English literature, so having mentioned the Christian gospels I need only mention a story added to them by the fathers of the Christian church: the story of the devil. This says God was *not* alone before he made the world but lived in the heaven of an earlier creation with lesser gods, his servants. One of these rebelled, was cast out with his followers, and became the devil. God then made people to serve him instead, but first made the world as a ground where he could first test their loyalty. The test was the rebel god, allowed by the strongest god to roam the world goading people into rebellion too.

No advantage of race, wealth or cleverness was needed to become Christian and the earliest commentators on Christianity say it was widespread among slaves and women: those whose lives the empire spectacularly cheapened. Roman justice, Roman triumphs and Roman circuses had turned organised cruelty and the murder of the helpless into civic duties, common conveniences and popular entertainments. Like the law in all countries Roman law was mainly devised to protect the property of those who had a lot and allow the owners to do what they liked with it. Roman law defined slaves and infants as property. How the Romans used slaves and prisoners of war in the Colosseum is well known. In the streets outside, inconvenient babies, mostly girls, were left in urns in public places to die or be picked up by those with a use for one. Rich people did this with their own surplus children: why not with the children of their slaves? It was sometimes cheaper to buy or inherit a working adult than pay to rear one from infancy. When Christianity was made the official religion of the empire many Christians attacked the temples and synagogues of their neighbours and fought each other over the nature of the man who told them to love their enemies; but if Gibbon is right in thinking Christianity destroyed that empire we should all thank God for it.

In the fourth century of the Christian era Saint Jerome translated the Jewish and Christian gospels into Latin, putting the Bible beside Virgil's Aeneid as the greatest classic of Latin literature. Monks and scholars copied and preserved them till the invention of printing, for though very different they inspired a similar hope. The Bible promised a future heaven, perhaps even a heaven on earth, for those who joined the pilgimage to the New Jerusalem which started when Moses led god's children out of Egypt. Virgil suggested that centuries of earthly warfare would one day end in a well-governed, peaceful kingdom for everyone. At the present time (Britain 1989) the idea that world history or any people's history can move toward a better state for all is widely advertised as socialist or utopian, but certainly impractical and out of date. Most prosperous people believe no better state is possible for anyone. This too will pass.

About 400 AD the Chinese empire had expanded beyond the wall built to protect it, displacing fierce nomads who suddenly invaded Europe from the east. The Roman empire had always been under threat from German tribes in the northern forests and these too now helped to break it up. Caesar Constantine had already shifted the capital from Rome to Byzantium, which became the centre of the biggest and richest region to survive the crack-up. Rome dwindled to a collection of vast half-empty buildings housing a Christian bishop. Elsewhere in Europe a few towns became separate communes ruled by Roman law but fed by traders who mainly bartered: outside such towns the only goverment was the protection of local war lords who taxed by plundering. Folk cannot be plundered continually unless allowed time to recover. From this social chaos grew feudal Europe: a collection of states whose fields, cottages and strongholds were not owned by the users but rented from a landlord who was ultimately a king. Rent was paid in produce or labour or war service, not money. Even in the towns money was only used as a means of exchange, so for nearly a millenium Christians thought money-lending for profit was an unnatural vice.

In Virgil's first pastoral poem a small farmer robbed of his land by the government laments that he and those like him must now disperse.

> To Scythia, bone-dry Africa, the chalky spate of the Oxus, Even to Britain, that place cut off at the very world's end.

Britain is now the home of nearly 56 million people, over nine-tenths of them in dense urban clusters. Of the remaining land nearly half is very fertile and supports mixtures of arable and cattle farming. The rest is mountain, hill, moorland and downs where very few folk live because it is used for sheep farms, military projects, cheap forestry and the sports of the wealthy. When Julius Caesar invaded Britain it housed about 600,000, and they dwelt mainly in the high valleys, the bays and islands round the coast, on the moorlands and downs whre the great stone monuments and earthworks stand. The land now occupied by our cities and agriculture was mostly swampy forest, for fertile soil near slow wide rivers can only be cultivated when the banks are made firm and the ground is drained. There was farming here but in clearings. The legions subdued Britain up to Pictland, though their hold on Wales and the north was slight and they did not touch Ireland. They built towns supported by villa farming and linked by roads which pierced the deciduous jungle. General Constantine was opposing the Picts in 306 AD when his father died and the troops proclaimed him Caesar. It was he who, without being christened, made Christianity the official Roman religion then moved the imperial capital east. Two and a half centuries later a historian and diplomat in

Constantinople wrote a book saying an area of Britain is under so thick a layer of snakes that none can stand there, some air so poisonous that none can breathe it. He says many think Britain a home of the dead, that boatmen on the French coast ferry ghosts by night across the narrow channel to the British shore. Like the planet Mars in the early twentieth century Britain had become a place of which anything could be imagined. The English were there.

The press of populations westward which drove tribes of fighters down into Italy, France and Spain had pushed other German tribes across the sea in ships. Their skill in woodcraft is proved by their ships, in metalwork by their weapons. In the Romanised Britain of the south and east they found woodlands like those they had left but without enough natives to support them as a ruling class. At home the Anglo-Saxon tribes only elected a king for the duration of a war. The wars establishing their settlements in Britain never ended because they were soon fighting or preparing to fight each other. Many little quarrelsome kingdoms were founded, six with the names and territories of modern English counties. Their wars created slaves as well as kings. The remaining Britons were forced out among the Celtic nations of the eastward coast, which was now called Wales. Rivers, homesteads and boundaries, even the days of the week were renamed in German and with names of northern gods who replaced the Celtic and Roman ones. What we now call the North Sea became a German sea with German tribes and kingdoms on its coasts from Norway down to France in the west, from Kent up to Edinburgh in the east. But the Germans in mainland Europe were being informed by the language and faith of those they conquered. In the lands lost by Roman Britain the British, Roman and Christian thought vanished as completely as the art of building with stone and brick.

But though the North Sea had become a German Mediterranean the Irish Sea was still a Celtic one, the kingdoms of Ireland on its west coast, the islands and penninsula of the Scots to the north, Strathclyde and Cumbria to the east, Cornwall to the south. These had been governed by alliances of tribal chieftains and a hereditary class of poetic law-makers who sang of the chieftains' prowess and judged their disputes. Without pressure of conquest the chieftains were now adopting Christianity, several of them becoming missionaries and priests. Monasteries were founded where monks copied Jerome's bible and other Latin classics while writing their own chronicles and poems in Gaelic as well as Latin. For two or three centuries before the Viking invasions knocked everything about, this Celtic Mediterranean was a safe place for scholarship. The cathedral island of Iona became its spiritual capital. Two seas and stormy new pagan kingdoms separated this Celtic church from the Roman one, which for a while had little time for peaceful scholarship. Mohammedan raiders were taking Africa and Spain away from Christianity; in north Europe the priesthood were helping the fierce gothic monarchies against Attila; the Roman and Byzantine bishops were quarrelling about the nature of the Holy Trinity: Irish-Scottish scholars had a high reputation around the Latin-Greek Mediterranean. Irish Celts founded monasteries in Burgundy and Switzerland. This Christian scholarship on the far side of a pagan wilderness encouraged the view of Britain as a dank dangerous forested place lit by supernatural gleams. The English settlers there had this view of life in general, when they came to write it down.

In the seventh century Northumbria became the biggest and most stable English kingdom, holding back Picts north of the Forth, Mercians south of the Humber, and driving the Welsh of Cumbria further into the west: yet it was Christianised by monks from Iona in what seems less than fifty years. At Jarrow, Wearmouth and the Holy Isle of Lindisfarne they and their pupils made gospel books in a style the *Encyclopaedia Britannica* calls Hiberno-Saxon, which means Irish-English. The initials of words were surrounded or filled with richly interwoven Celtic scrolls and spirals, skilfully inlaid with gold and the jewelled colours the Anglo-Saxons used in their finest metal ornaments. Remember a piece of music, or a building, or machine, or anything which gave you delight along with astonishment that people could make it. Pages of the Book of Kells and the Lindisfarne Gospel are as good as that. Until the 9th century such books, with church ornaments of metal and ivory, were Britain's only notable export - the continental clergy wanted them. And at Whitby in a monastery with a Gaelic name (Streaneshalch) the new Christian learning stirred two very different people into making the first English literature.

Hilda's uncle was a pagan Northumbrian king, a successful warlord who gave his name (Edwin) to his northern capital (Edinburgh). He got baptised five years before he died and Hilda, then thirteen, was baptised with him. She became a nun, an abbess and a saint, after ruling the double monastery for nuns and monks at Whitby. While working there she learnt that a local herdsman thought he was a poet, though he had not composed anything. An angel in a dream had ordered him to sing about "the beginning of things", but he was too ignorant to start. Hilda tested the man's talent by getting priests to tell him the Christian creation story and to write down what he made of it. His verses were good. He never learnt to write but was enrolled in the monastery where he dictated more poems.

Any talent which gives a good new thing to others is a miracle, but commentators have thought it extra-miraculous that England's first known poet was an illiterate herd. They forgot three things:

1. Poetry is a kind of speech, not a kind of writing. For over half a million years poets learned to make it by hearing it sung or recited, then by repeating it with the changes and additions they preferred. In a very few places, three or four thousand years ago, writing approached poetry as a humble secretary, able to record an especially good poem so that later folk could not change or lose it. The vulgar notion that a poet must be a writer arrived when a lot of wealthy literate folk decided nothing good could be made without the help of their expensive educations, except by a miracle. In Hilda's day even emperors could not write. Nobody expected it of a poet.

2. After hearing and repeating poems until the rhythms and the vocabularies are in their nerves, poets need long uninterrupted spells of talking to themselves. Herding once allowed this. From Theocritus in ancient Greece to James Hogg twenty centuries later, the link between herding and poetry was so famous a literary cliche that even writers forgot it had been a fact.

3. The miracle was a clever strong ruler using her learning and advantages to free a poet in the slave class. With more like Hilda literature would not now contain such huge silences and absences about the lives of most people. She really was a saint.

So now English literature can start. A monk who got learning from the Irish Scots is taking dictation from a herdsman singing to him in a Northumbrian dialect of Anglo-Saxon. He sings a Jewish creation story transmitted to him through at least three other languages by a Graeco-Roman-Celtic Christian church. Since the verse forms and vocabularies in his nerves were learnt from pagan German warrior chants, his Genesis poem is colder, fiercer and more spooky than the version we know: the version authorised by a Tudor head of state nearly a thousand years later. This is also because he prefaces his Genesis with the story of how God's chief angel became the devil. The monk writing this uses an alphabet close to our own, a Roman adaptation of a Greek adaptation of a Semitic adaptation of an Egyptian adaptation of signs used first beside the Euphrates river in the city of Sumer, later called Babylon, five thousand years before Christ. To give you a taste of the language the poet and the monk used, here is Christ's best-known prayer in Anglo-Saxon, with the better-known Tudor English version beside it.

Christ's Prayer: c650

Faeder ure,
Thu the eart heafonum,
Si thin nama gehalgod.
Tobecume thin rice.
Gewurthe thin will on eorthan
   swa swa on heofonum.
Urne gedaeghwamlican
   hlaf syle us to daeg
And forgyf us ure gyltas
  swa swa we forgyfath
   ure gyltendum
And ne gelaed thu us on costnunge,
Ac alys us of yfele.
Sothlice.

Christ's Prayer: c1550

Our father,
Whyche art in heaven,
Halowed be thy name.
Thy Kyngdome come.
Thy wyll be doen in yearth
   as it is in heaven.
Geve us this daye
   our dayly breade.
And forgeve us our trespaces,
  as wee forgeve them
   that trespasse agaynst us.
And leade us not into temptacion.
But deliver us from evill.
Amen.

All these old English words contain sounds of words we still use, apart from *rice* (realm, or *reich* in German) and *sothlice* (truth-like or truly). Gewurthe means, worth be given; the unwieldy *gedaeghwamlican* has daily inside: *hlaf* means loaf: *gyltas* guilt: *Gyltendum*, guilty-doers-to: *costnunge*, a bad or costly choice: *alys*, release. If spoken in some northern accents it sounds oddly familiar. Some folk still say "oor faither" and "thoo art".

Alasdair Gray

(Note: this is an extract from the introduction to Alasdair Gray's Anthology of Prefaces *to be published in due course by Canongate, although with the introduction in a slightly different form.)*

Raymond Vettese

WILLIE'S TREE

At the end o the green a sycamore
spreids muckle brainches. I canna dismiss
ae thocht as I lounge in heat o simmer,
glaid o shade: Willie Soutar planted this.

Aince it wisna tree ava, juist a skelf,
a scrimpit thing, but noo it's undaunted
and hauds tae heiven the strength o its years,
the sycamore Willie Soutar planted.

Willie's awa, Willie's lang laid doon,
but the seeds in the wind gaed blawin free
and rooted themsels, thrust deep in the land.
Whanever birds sing, it's on Willie's tree.

A PROPER STEEL

I cast my thochts back til oor nichts o fire
whaun the bluid wad oot, ay, and the het seed;
the haill warl spun on the rod o desire
and spirt o word flooded in tide o deed.
That wis needfu then, cuidna be ither,
and we'd thole ocht, be it bench or beach-dune,
for the kinnlin moment's heat thegither.
Love, then, wis drums, no a fiddler's douce tune.
But that wis lang syne, lang syne. The need crines.
As onie fire burns doon and disna lowe
sae muckle as aince it did, sae lust dwines,
wan as the muin or blue flames that rowe
abuin sea-coals, haurdly seen whiles. And yet
something bides. It's no the fury o youth,
that's gane. For mysel I dinna regret
the passion o then, but here's a new truth
in place o sic demand, a love that kens
itsel, that disna need proofs, the constant
couplin, but raither on quietness depen's.
No quiet withoot onie thocht or want,
but quiet that's been thro the fire an's hardened
til a proper steel, winna brak ava,
furnaced and milled thro monie fauts pardoned.
Here's nae spunk-stairch easy dichted awa
but's love layered til a deepness o strength
never meisured by the brief-thrabbin length.

THE DAITHWATCH

As common, as difficult a thing, as birth;
as common, as haurd a thing, as pain.
And you, in the hairt o this,
suffert. As common a thing as rain
oor tears, as common as braith
or the bluid that rises frae a wound,
only that we oor lane must thole
this raxin stound,
common as gress or a lover's kiss.
Whit mair's tae be said? Mebbe nocht.
As common, as difficult a thing, as birth,
but oot o this sicna grief is wrocht,
as difficult as faith, as common as yirth.

AMANG THE SHADDAS

Ae Christmas Eve my faither tippied in
and I, no asleep, throu my hauf-shut een,
saw him lay doon the presents that wad be
Santie's the morn. Yon didna fash me.
I'd been shair, or near shair, for a while,
that the twa were ane. I said nocht, never
let on, and as I grew aulder the tale
juist drappit awa frae thocht, slowly deed
by silences, never talked o again.

I think o that whaun you spier me o God.
I dinna believe. I'm shair, or near shair.
Yon tale, for me, has juist drappit awa,
gane oot o thocht. Only whaun sic as you
deave me for a proof div I own its lack
ae wye or tither, and ken I canna
draa owre muckle like atween my faither
and this, for wha, tho waukrife an' watchfu,
will see God ploiter amang the shaddas?

VOYAGE

Whit wis the end o your voyage
grandfaither? Wis it here, truly,
in a cauld lan' sae faur awa
frae the ripe vinyairds o youth-heid?
Or wis that country aye in mind,
the journey back, tho never taen,

the true end o your lang trauchle?
I dinna ken, I canna speak for you,
only mysel, your grandson in
Scotland, wha speaks an' writes in a
tongue you never maistered. Is it
in me, in us, the hairst o your
seed, that you are syne fu-gaithert?
I dinna ken, but whiles think o
Italy as the fremd country whaurin
my deepest roots drive, and whiles o
Scotland as the country we've been
somehoo driven til, for whitna ettle
I amna shair, lessen it's tae complete
a journey o the flesh by gien it
the spreit o meanin, the bairns that growe
frae coorse grun' the wine o celebration
and press frae your darg the joy that,
spiced wi a dose o guid Scottish smeddum,
gies mebbe the richt mix o strengths:
a gless o waarm sooth wi north ice in't.

EPITAPH

Scotland bore me, bored me,
donnert an' scunnert me,
but at the lowse hauds me,
tho I grudge it and it grudge me.

TOURIST GUIDE

Whitna need tae gang til Pompeii
for a fowk an' a place turnt stane?
In Scotland ye'll find, gin ye stay behind,
we fossilise oor ain.

WASHED-OOT

The ink's dried in the pen,
for tho the nib's sair-pressed
nocht comes.
Nae pity for the poet.
Anither lifts the pen
and the blue floods
glisten and the tide
rins fresh.

In a drumlie pool
unstirred by ocht
a drained face goaves,
ravaged as the muin
and as deid.

THE SEA'S NOISE

The sea's noise in a white shell's lug -
flindert partans bruckle aneath
oor dacklin feet at the tide's lip,
amang weed an' twig, rotten floats,
plaistic bottles, cans, the blue-white
mosaic o mussel rissoms.
Salmon nets stilpin oot on stilts
t'wards the horizon and gows
greetin abuin as we hunker howkin
eels whaur the shed skin o waater glistens.
The sea's noise in a white shell's lug
and oor shuin gritted fu o saun
we cairted hame an' mither's skelp
for the scunner o it, the lugs
roarin syne wi dirlin het pain,
hurt bluid's noise in a lug's reid shell.

THE PERMANENCE ALOW

Lang syne we'd mist the gless
and write oor names,
but yon aye soon faded.

Noo, years aifter, we ken
love canna be
ghaisted frae wishfu braith.

We've howked thro surface's
bricht deception
to permanence alow

whaur love can be written
on ilka deed,
on ilka day, and bides.

ON LEAVING TEACHING

Ten year I did, ten lang year, but nae mair!
Joy is that maist simple o things -
the kennin that ane can still dare
despite age and the voice that brings
ocht-day sense richt up til the fore.
Hing the pension and thocht o the morn!
I'm aff like onie haflin til the splore.
Wha kens whitna byspale's aboot tae be born?

SILENCE AND FIRE

By the pool's side at noon we lay,
in the green tree's shade, and said nocht.
I heard sauchs stir and a fish lowp
and the chirmin birds wadna hae
silence. But oh we wad. We lay
silent and I thocht o silence
or it seemed that rays o silence
like stour-crossed beams thrust oot o us.
We gied oot silence as the sun
gies oot heat, and the silent heat
flamed us baith or wi no a word
spoken we turnt til each ither
and silence and fire became love,
and then nae ither soond I heard
(tho dootless the warl made its noise)
but the stoundin hairt and the bluid's roar.

TAK THE MOMENT

The stars will never disappear,
only us, already e'en noo
hauf-wey intil the howe o dairk
wi nae stars ava. Ach, let be
sic dowie thochts, tak the moment
as it flees an' let's bide a while
immortal as the galaxies
aye hae been, whether true or no,
til the poets and the lovers.
Lie aneath stars wi Helen, Paris,
afore the fated rooftaps burn.

Raymond Vettese

Fergus Chadwick

MINERVA IN THE IVY

Sour ivy, black purple fruits,
poison hard as grapeshot
in scaly mantles of leaves
whose pale lightning crazes the green.

She says, Let poor birds eat
this cake. There is nothing else:
only these clusters, agate beads
shielded by hawthorn thickets
where the owl's turret softly turns
in the fog and its white lies.

No fruit save the hard to swallow:
nothing moves, it is guerrilla war,
maximum night.

The army of hunger and rags
goes by, loots and litters dry woods,
junk ditches, X-ray stalks, dingy scrub,
the crimson of winter briars
stitched tight as razor scars.

A ghost grooms in grey mirrors
hung with the sleep of lesser birds.
An idol wakes, unbribable
as death under the glitzy sky.

PEGASUS

The stables are empty. Very high,
through fingers held against the blue,
something moves, a silver snip.

Calmly squeezing tunnels of vapour,
the white haunches shudder,
seal-smooth, and push thinnest airwaves.

Shoes with buckles pace to the door
again; clatter involuntary hoofs
where swallows once messed the sills.

But no one can cling to his back,
no rider; each blown off by wing-beats
crawls on this dungeon straw,

Watched by the long-lashed eyes of nags;
but he, legs tucked, a toy-soldier's horse,
wins even higher altitudes.

The stalls have that horse-bum smell,
which the lads forking barrows
of manure breathe in and hire out.

Their art is comb-and-paper
music, suspicious of the shoes
whose stiff ears twitch, vulnerable

Every mile of the road; every breath
that jets in a colder air miming
for the sidewinder that purer trail.

HUNTER GATHERER

I stumbled like a dense seeker
painting darkness with his smoky torch,
and fell into the cave.
Black as lamplit eyes,
the live rock flexing bulls.
My hands spoke their forbidden language,
it was *my* skin arrows pierced.

Curious, as to the dead, why
their lipless screams resembled
sexual grins, it was proved to me
how corpse hands, dragging,
gripped the sand.

I feared those wicker baskets
crammed with living dead.
The neat huts row on row.
There *is* evil. These
are its rotten fruit; corpses
piled in their mnemonic rings.

THE EMPEROR'S ROSE-PETAL DIG

What are they like, the dead days,
all the days gone, packed mille-feuille
together, the moments, childhood
seen again, granted the axe to cut?

Granted review, if our lives
weren't rose's crockery, weren't
moments which forget their decision
to last, stuffed like rose-petals now

In the deadwood rubbish-dump
layered with wet-buckled leaves.
My ghost the inheritor then.
The inheritor of these moments

Lost to research, outside the dig,
looks at my life. Does it see
an old toolshed with oak flowers
in dust, & reefed cobwebs in the close air?

Directories of the days,
my love in three volumes, stuck
fast with the glue of time's pressure.
Who knows if my body wore this mask,

Pledged before it left the tribe
of childhood not to recognise
the armfuls of its own joys?
Tiberius calls for his skull again,

And wakes, shocked out of the earth,
the sun a cloudy island of flame,
and hears the bark on his skin
wrenched whole from his cork-oak side.

RECEIVING A TRAITOR'S LEG, PERTH, 1305

Quarters received at Perth;
Newcastle; Stirling; Berwick . . .
Not my job to say this isn't
a quarter, only a naked leg
with some buttock pertaining.
Think of the way it's come
(or rather don't); the hessian
sack loosely tied, studded
with flies; labelled 'Wallace,
one quarter to Perth', et cetera.
Dogs must've eaten the toes.
What a stink, lolloping
to and fro in a red cart . . .
Hammer it onto the spike,
then; stand back; a rich sight.
Pearly maggots escaping
drip from the hero's wounds.
Run, crook leg, run away now
if you can, poor bastard, Wallace.
Nowhere now to cross your legs
under oaken tables of state,
your foot-pulse twitching damask.
Dancing flies, and many wings
fan a black wafting stench . . .
Why me that always gets this job?
Nobody owns this rotting leg.
Mine, the last hand, runs up it

slowly in a sighing stroke.
Where its twin is, God knows;
Stirling probably, days' travel
inbetween the fork girls eyed.
His legs then spun a reel,
a full calf flexing proud and white;
stockinged feet landing no more
than an instant on fire-lit boards
that jumped with whooping rhythm!
Is this a man? Is this like mine?
My legs move, one after the other
downwards, round the spiral stairs.

Fergus Chadwick

Fred Johnston

MIDDLE DISTANCE

(for my daughter, Saoirse Deirdre)

Look into the middle distance:
from that small scarce discerned point
we are born

all the long-view philosophies dry up
(the heart's lens is stronger)
I'd stare into the sea any day

rather than scrape around in bookshops
for something to lean on:
shelves into infinity, larger than life

I know them, the instant poets
celebrities of verse, photogenic
subject to no laws now -

but in the middle distance, where
the song of children is an anthem,
where new-cut grass covers the plain

and the slopes of hills are holy again -
this, out of the neon glare of security,
out of the rattle and crash of banks

this is the true horizon - look, daughter,
the rain runs differently here,
the weekend poetry of cities dies away

into the middle distance we stare
as into a new rising sun - in the mind's
eye ungovernable poetry constructs

itself, without permission, without style,
a path cut by weather's work
not the cowardice of diggers and tar

lean on the West wind, where
birds lean, where storms lean too:
breathe a cleaner air, wish on a star.

HOMER

I knew blind Homer, he
of night cafés and cups of tea

who sang in dole-queues; sang,
for whom the very pay-hatch rang

and he of Kavanagh, whose lilt
caressed the stones as walls were built

who paid for drink in verse
and died of grieving when grief was scarce:

one more who begged for fags
carrying assorted shopping-bags

drowned in a winter's tide
a bag-hugging, fagless old suicide -

the one I fear most is me
condemned to visions of the other three

as I dribble, old, alone,
coming at last to claim their own.

TO ELENA SANCHEZ

In Spain, you say,
poetry is a gift from God:
here, it is a curse,
a maker of false distinctions
it separates and divides
provides prophets
and outcasts
and no woman will marry
a poet
whose shirt is not silk -

do not trap me with those
Granada eyes
or tell me I have a gift
from God

for the owner of this café,
in his own way gifted,
eats more regularly than I,
is a son of the city,
and has never queued
for a hand-out in his life -

In Spain, Elena, would I see
a different sun,
honey-coloured, my arms
and legs,
roses in my teeth?
Would I wear a straw hat
in Summer and sit in the
shade of orange trees,
peeling off poems until
the soft core of myself
seeped through?

ADAM'S DREAM

Outside this garden, what am I?
All painless pleasure
time going by without me,
I am idle and long for change

for the company of pipe-smoking
thinking men, a good cigar
and decent conversation
men to whom my life is strange

compared to theirs. A single
sunrise, this, waking
to a pain in my side, out of
dreams of apples and snakes

I am unprepared, unread,
untried, and something tells me
that, despite a strong arm and
continued comfort, I lack what it takes:

I am a gardener, but the flowers
do not need me; a shepherd, but
the herds never stray; a hunter,
but fruit falls into my hands

I crave the yap of children
their curiosity and fun -
I am frightened, I am lonely,
and no-one understands.

Fred Johnston

The Moon and Me
Anne Hay

A battered green Commer van appeared round the bend in the road. Shiona and Ruth jumped down from their seat on the wall. The driver came round to open up the back and they climbed in. Inside were planks placed on bricks, which wobbled until the van went its round of the housing estate and the places filled up with the weight of a dozen sleepy adolescents. Above the low chatter a boy sang 'Get back, get back, get back to where you once belonged.' over and over again, the same few bars, in a mid-Atlantic accent quite unlike his own speaking voice.

"Shut up!"

"S'a free country."

In the background BBC radio murmured the news. At the same time as the van passed through Luncarty and turned off the A9 towards the farm, Apollo 11 was making its ascent (or descent, depending on your point of view) towards the surface of the moon.

Shiona wasn't listening. She was counting, inside her head. Today she wanted to go home with a note. Not just a few half-crowns and shillings for a day's work. She imagined herself unfolding it, later in the day, to show Mum and Catriona. But for ten bob, at tuppence a pound, you had to pick sixty pounds of raspberries, that was a hundred and twenty punnets. She could do it, at a push.

Once they'd gone through Stanley, they were almost there. When they clambered out into the daylight again, the ground was still damp from last night's rain, and threw up a sweet, earthy smell. The company trooped down the farm track towards the berry dreels. Kevin was already unloading the crates from the tractor. The sun was beginning to warm the cool morning air.

Shiona collected her plastic baskets and tied them round her waist with a piece of string from her anorak pocket.

"Mine's burst, Mr Fauldburn!" called Ruth.

The farmer slowly took a tangled ball of string from the front of the tractor, and a knife from his pocket. He measured her waist with his eyes and the string with his hands, and cut it.

"That'll be enough for your wee waist," he winked and widened his smile, putting the length round her waist to try it. It was correct to within two inches. He rolled it up and placed it in her hand.

"Thanks." Ruth's face was completely hidden by two sheafs of hair, separated by a centre parting, which met in the middle when she bent her head. Then she looked up, smiled back, and turned to walk away with a self-conscious wiggle of her hips.

They stood in line to collect their crates, filled them with a pile of white cardboard punnets and walked down the track to where the day's picking was. They placed the crates at the end of the dreel, placed the white punnets, two in each plastic basket tied around their waist. Their hands free, they started to pick.

The bushes were wet and soaked their hands and cuffs when they searched under the leaves for the ripe fruit. On their hands and wrists was a tracery of new scratches, red hairline scabs from yesterday's scratches, and thin marks where the scabs had fallen and left thin white streaks on their brown skin. You had to work fast. Seventy punnets by lunchtime, Shiona set herself. Easy. The bushes were heavy with fruit.

An ache in her stomach started mid-morning. She shivered. The sun was rising and the bushes were drying. Her crate was gradually filling up with red.

"C'mon boys, back to work, it's only piece-time, not lunchtime." A gruff voice floated over from half-a-dozen dreels away. The girls never stopped for piece-time. It was a waste. Anyway, Shiona and Ruth talked all day long. It wasn't like school. You could talk all you wanted. And get paid for it. Shiona liked having Ruth all to herself. She knew a lot of things. Not the things you learn in school. The other things. Ruth was the youngest of three, Shiona was the eldest of two. Ruth was the first in their group to wear a bra, kiss a boy, start her periods. Or so she said.

The first crate was full. "Give's a lift, Ruth." They put one hand in the handle each side of the crate, balanced it and walked up to the tractor. Kevin lifted it (all by himself) onto the scales.

"Over." He took the top berries out of each punnet into two fresh ones to even them all up and tip the scales right. Then he took out a grubby notebook and wrote down some figures.

They walked back to the dreel with an empty crate. Shiona was pleased. A two-punnet start to her next crate. Back at the dreel she popped a sun-warmed berry into her mouth. That was when the fruit tasted best. Warm, ripe, red, bursting into your mouth with the taste of summer.

The whistle blew at twelve. Pickers emerged from dreels like weary creatures climbing out of air-raid shelters on the all-clear. They settled down on groundsheets and unpacked food from satchels. A picnic every day was one of the attractions. Shiona ate a sandwich and a half and felt slightly queasy. An excited shudder seemed to move inside her. She packed the rest away in her bag in case she was hungry later, and set off down the track.

The pickers' toilet was two strawberry fields away. Shiona went for the walk sometimes, whether she needed to or not. It was good to be alone, to feel and hear and listen and pretend. She kept close to the edge of the field so as not to trample on the growing bushes. The sun beat down upon her neck, gulls cried overhead. She imagined herself as a girl in a story, dressed in a floating white dress and a hat trimmed with fresh flowers, carrying a parasol, walking through fields of wind-blown wheat.

The toilet was a tiny shed you could stand up in and no more, with a wooden plank laid up against the door to indicate it was empty. She lifted the plank, laid it aside, and opened the door. The smell hit her. Flies buzzed. It was only a hole in the ground that the farmer dug and filled up once the season was over. A sort of commode was built over it and torn-up magazines hung from a string in the corner. She sat on the seat carefully, checking it for splinters.

Then she made the discovery. An unmistakable red stain. What she'd waited months for. She stared at it in sudden panic. She checked her trousers. It hadn't gone through. If only Mum was there. Back through the fields she ran, not seeing the strawberry bushes or hearing gulls call, or feeling the white dress swish.

Ruth gasped. "You'd better go and see Mrs Fauldburn. She'll know what to do."

Of course. Good idea. Mrs Fauldburn was somebody's mother.

She passed the tractor on the way to the farmhouse.

"All right?" called Mr Fauldburn. Kevin was looking, too.

"I just want to see Mrs Fauldburn." Her face burned red. The farmer nodded and said nothing. Kevin's face had that vacant look about it.

She banged the knocker on the big open farmhouse door.

"In here, in the kitchen," called a voice from the back of the house.

The house smelt of dust and wet dog, and then of a sugary warm smell, boiling jam coming from the same direction as the voice.

"Hello love, what can I do for you?" Mrs Fauldburn was spooning pinkish-white scum from the top of the jelly-pan.

Shiona blurted out, "My period's come."

"Oh. Do you want a sanny? Come on up."

"It's my first one," Shiona confessed, following Mrs Fauldburn's wide bottom up creaky stairs. She felt tears gathering in the corner of her eyes.

"Oh dear, love." The woman turned round on the landing and gave her a hug. Shiona jerked rigid at the sudden closeness of so much hot, sweating flesh. Mrs Fauldburn disappeared into a bedroom and Shiona waited. Everything seemed to be brown and a hundred years old. It was the sort of house you'd be scared to go to sleep in at night. She preferred a clean semi smelling of things like Flash.

"These were Sandra's." Mrs Fauldburn handed her a sanitary belt and a stretched pair of knickers and a white pad smelling of mothballs. "Go in there if you want to sort yourself out. Can you manage?"

The bathroom was ancient too. She sat on the wooden toilet seat and tried to work out what to do with all the bits. The lady supervisor had shown them at school, but that was about two years ago. She took off her trousers and pants, managed to attach the belt to the pad, and dressed again. She stuffed the soiled pants into her pocket. She checked in the mirror to see if there were any bulges. She wasn't sure there wasn't.

Back down in the kitchen Mrs Fauldburn was checking her jam.

"All right?"

"All right, thanks."

"Sure you don't need a wee aspirin?"

"No thanks. I'll just get along back."

She walked back to the dreels. The pad felt as if it reached half-way down to her knees. It was held together with something like soft barbed wire. Comfortable enough as long as you didn't want to move. She sighed. She could have sworn that Mr Fauldburn and Kevin, standing rolling cigarettes by the tractor, had X-ray eyes.

Ruth was already picking. Shiona's hands started to move quickly, to catch up to the same part of the bush.

"You all right?"

"She fixed you up?"

"Yes."

"Poor you. I bet you wish you could go home."

"No I don't."

She wanted to ask if it was supposed to feel so horrible, but it would be childish and she already lagged behind by not starting till thirteen. Anyway, she had to concentrate on the berries still to be picked. She couldn't go home until the van did, so she might as well make the most of it. She still wanted that ten bob note or the day was going to be completely ruined.

The sun scorched its way across the sky. The girls worked steadily, swapping confidences over the bushes as the chorus of 'Get Back' floated over from the next dreel.

"Ruth."

"Yeah?"

"Do you use these Tampax?"

"I tried one. I couldn't get it in right. My mum says you should really wait till you're married."

A hard pink berry came flying over the bush. There was silence. Shiona suddenly realised the singing had stopped. She heard giggling. The boys were right behind them, though they were so short you couldn't see their heads over the bushes.

"Stupid little boys shouldn't listen to big girls' conversations," shouted Ruth, and put a berry in her mouth. Shiona wanted to die.

The whole thing was disgusting. Sometimes, moving, she felt a rush of blood. Panic took her. Supposing it overflowed and trickled down her leg? It was unbelievably disgusting, despite what the lady supervisor had said about that bit of you having less germs than your mouth. Imagine all those women walking around the place with blood-soaked bits of cotton-wool between their legs. All that every month until you were old, and just so you could have a couple of babies. What a waste for all the women who didn't have any children and had to go through all this every month for nothing. Every month. From thirteen, till, say, thirty-three or whenever you were too old, that was twenty years. Times twelve made it two hundred and forty. Two hundred and forty periods! An hour was enough. She wanted to tear the thing off and throw it away.

It was five to four, just before the whistle went, when she filled her last crate. The girls staggered up to the tractor, stood in the queue for weighing the last of the day's pickings. Kevin weighed, Mr Fauldburn totted up the figures in his notebook and gave out the money. Shiona's last crate just tipped the scales at the right amount. "Ten shillings and tuppence," he called out. She had a sudden fear he might give her coins, but she saw him reach into his back pocket and bring out a new red note.

"You're some worker for your size," he said, handing her the note and the copper. She waited. Ruth got nine and tuppence.

They sat almost in silence in the van on the way home. It was a special silence. The quiet and stillness of rest after a long day's work. Though some of the boys chattered, and yawned loudly, and 'Get Back' still whistled.

Shiona jumped off the van at the bottom of the road and waved. She checked her pocket for the money, and dragged her body up the long hill to her house. When she went in Mum and Catriona were watching television. She'd forgotten! The moon landing! The set flickered with black-and-white pictures of men moving in slow motion in an eerie, dusty landscape.

"You missed most of it," said Catriona with obvious satisfaction. Shiona made a face back at her and sat down.

They'd put up a flag.

"How does the flag fly if there's no wind?"

"There's a stick along the top to hold it up. You can see that," replied her sister, in a really irritating way.

"Well," said her mother, turning away from the moon for a moment, "how did you get on?"

She took the note out of her pocket, and, as she had imagined, unrolled it and held it up. No-one was looking. "I made ten shillings," she announced.

"Very good." Her mother's reaction was somehow less than she had expected. Catriona still ignored her. The two men moved like inflated puppets. All that distance. Away up there. If man could land on the moon, he could do anything. There would be no more wars on earth, they would just fight it all out in space, where nobody would get hurt.

A soggy feeling brought her back to earth. "Mum."

"Uhuh."

"Eh . . ." She didn't want to speak in front of Catriona. "Can I talk to you about something?"

"Yes, go on."

"It's . . . you know . . . it's happened." Catriona, who'd not heard a word about the ten shilling note, swivelled her head round immediately.

Her mother looked blank for a moment, then followed her through to the hall. She told her. About the bloodstain, going to see Mrs Fauldburn, and wearing Mrs Fauldburn's daughter's knickers. Her mother looked shocked, as if it wasn't something that was bound to happen sooner or later, but then she recovered herself and went to fetch the packet of towels that had gone with them each summer holiday to Carnoustie. Shiona sorted herself up and went back through to the living-room. She felt tears pricking the back of her eyes again. She was tired and uncomfortable, and something else, a sort of edgy feeling as if she couldn't sit down. She had a momentary pang of envy for Catriona, sitting on the floor with a pair of Mum's high heels on, playing a simple game of being grown up.

Dad came home and sat in front of the television, engrossed.

"I never thought I would see this," he enthused. "Look, Shiona, Catriona, look carefully, remember this. This is a day you'll remember for the rest of your lives." Tears started to roll down Shiona's cheeks, big, unstoppable tears that dripped off her chin onto her teeshirt. A great sob came out of her. Her father turned round, surprised.

"What have I said now?"

Her mother came through from the kitchen.

"Shiona's crying, Mum, I don't know why."

"Honestly, I didn't say a bloody word." Her father sighed and took out a cigarette packet from his jacket pocket. She leapt up and ran out of the room, slamming the door.

Her mother came up after a couple of minutes. Shiona was lying on the bed. Her mother sat down quietly beside her.

"It's all right. I've told him. He understands. Come on, I'll run you a bath. That's what you need, a nice hot bath."

That night, when she closed her eyes, all she could see were berries, millions of them, red berries, nestling behind green leaves. Her brain was still picking them. She shifted position. It was horrible having to sleep with that thing between your legs. Her mother had laid a towel across the bottom sheet, just in case.

She got out of bed, opened the curtains and looked at the moon. It looked just the same as it always did. She wondered how many people were looking out at the moon tonight. Supposing nobody had been there? Supposing they'd made it all up and the pictures were a fake? No. They thought they'd conquered it, but they hadn't. All they'd done was put up a flag and bring home a few handfuls of moondust. It still lay out there in space making the tides turn and wolves howl and your periods come, if you believed what they said.

It's a special day, she thought, slipping back between the sheets. For the moon and me. But we're still the same, really. Nothing's changed. And she lay down and slept the swift, deep sleep of a child.   Anne Hay

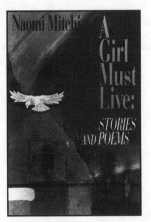

George Faludy
Translations by Thomas Land

*George Faludy: b. 1910, probably the greatest living Hungarian poet.
He recently returned to his native land after more than three
decades of self-imposed exile to receive a tumultuous welcome.*

MICHELANGELO'S FINAL PRAYER

Your arm describes the sun's curved course while standing
beside the earth, your anvil and domain.
For eighty-six years, I've sought understanding
upon the scaffolding, my Lord, in vain.

I'm left with lifeless forms or idols moulded
beneath my chisel from the crumbling blocks -
Your fleeting rainbow has remained unfolded
which grows beyond my reach within the rocks

Though I've become the marble, violated
by every storm, rough, mute and isolated -
my soul reflects the light which You have shone.

How can I cast aside the body's inner
confines? If You still love an ageing sinner,
strike here, great Master Sculptor! I'm the stone.

IBN AMAR AL-ANDALUSIA
(11th Century)

A hundred libraries and parks surrounded
the university where mosques and fountains
and jasmine, myrrh and passion's honey scent and
night revellers mingled with the olive trees.
His sword was fine, his charger black as ravens.
The Grand Vizier was quoted with devotion
by all Seville. He grew a little vain and
thus came to write his lyrics in this fashion:

*"Amar am I - my poetry's reputation
is carried by the winds and celebrated
beyond the deserts' dust, beyond the oceans' spray.
None but a fool knows not my name and station.
I am a golden lizard venerated
in golden sunshine. Whispering lovers say
my rhymes: the women melt through my creation.
My verse will go on, still disseminated -
still, even after I have passed away."*

And he was cheerful, happier than I
for time had not yet marked the fading Moresques
although the walls began to shed their plaster.
He did not know that men degenerate
and could not guess that one day soon the fountains
would wither short of water, dry and gaping.
He failed to see the weeds along the roads,
the rise of rubbish shrouding his horizon -
and to foresee the burning of the books,
the slaughter of the lovers of his rhyme -
and to perceive that neither rhymes nor gold
nor thought nor deed nor craft nor knife nor rage
nor rational conviction can support
a culture when it crumbles from decay.

CAFÉ FLORE

I HAD been drawn to this place from the start.
And here I dwelt, beside a glass of brandy,
back in my self-important student days
when I could always buy another *fine* but
just now and then I could not afford a meal.
And I thought I was made of fireworks.
Picasso sat here with his Spanish woman,
his back against the back wall of the room;
we nodded and I tried to write a poem
but it refused to gel. A homely place,
this modest, red Parisian one-room café,
its tiny glass-cage winter garden set
upon the boulevard. Full of arrogance,
young people entered (they were hissing rockets
just like myself) and some slid up the steep
dark stairs, some sat alone, some joined my table
- Starker, Mehring, Sinkó, Forgács, Havas,
Hevesi, Ney, Remenyik, Faragó -
and thus we chatted or talked politics
or simply sat in silence; but whatever
we did, we watched the quick revolving door
disgorging new arrivals, reinforcements,
the vanguard of the future from beyond
the realm of meagre present - and young women!
Girl students from as far as Burma, Thailand -
they'd come to choose new lovers but they seemed
to muse behind their long eyelashes over
the negative eight virtues of Gautama;
and energetic English girls in green,
displaying freckles wrought in copper, with

the proud proportions of a Roman goddess
but marred by clumsy movements - they often carried
enormous handbags used as barricades
against this world which they would never fathom
with either mind or body; and the girls
from Eastern Europe, lost in loud debate
with their escorts about the world's affairs
and under catchwords like materialism
they sought the spirit; and the girls of Paris!
slim, graceful and perhaps a trifle ugly,
they had learned all about life in the womb
and they were ready for life and against life,
these girls who had their taste and knew their fashion,
who wholly merged a tenderness and toughness
like well baked bread (and not like layered cake) -
each of them seemed complete and separate,
a planet bound by its own course and purpose
and full of self-awareness, will and pride.
I marvelled at these girls, as did the others.

OUR ELDERS also gathered here of an evening
- Julien Benda, Hatvani, Bréton
Werfel and once Roger Martin du Gard -
and after they had talked enough together
they called us to their table for a chat.
We learned from them and held them in esteem and
made mock of them behind their backs - they threw us
their guarded looks while whispering about us,
we turned away while whispering about them
for we had different manners having joined
the earthly table after the nineteenth century.
They knew that we were wet-nosed idiots
confused and rash and unreliable;
they knew the fragrance of our perspiration
and knew that we kicked up our heels too high
and that we smiled and panted at the same time
and that our smiles would freeze and break in time -
they envied us our smiles as yet unfrozen,
and winced at our trampling underfoot the polished,
blue marble slabs between the colonnades
without a backward glance, they thought we would
not notice if the structure should collapse
behind us and its fall might even please us.
They envied us for we would take possession,
excluding them, and shape the future and
could lightly cast their names aside at will
and even purge our skulls of memories
connected with them as you suppress a headache

without a pill. Together or alone
we sat, and they too watched the door revolving
admitting life's parade in intermittent
and single file. And they begrudged us in silence.
They envied us the ocean's sandy beaches,
our hundred future barefoot runs along
the shores avoiding the knives of cockle shells
until we'd stop to watch the breakers rear up,
white mares caressed by salty winds and sunshine,
to fall upon their knees before our feet;
they envied us our quiet walks in winter
along the fields of freshly fallen snow
or in the depths of early evenings when
the light's uncertain in the squalid lanes of
determination; and they envied us
the very fruits of trees and fields and sky,
the orange of the sun, the moon-banana,
our one-room attic homes with creaking floors;
they envied us the oil-lamps of love
with burning wicks that never can turn backwards,
the flames that burn but cannot ever scorch,
the force that will escape from all enforcement;
they envied us our solitary evenings
absorbed in books, the honey scented winds
of thirty gold acacia openings, our
still perfect, uncorroded blade of youth.

HOW OFTEN did I sit here with two wives,
three mistresses and with my many friends!
A purple mist spreads over St Germain:
no autumn fog - polluted summer air.
Une fine, Armand! Today I am alone.
I watch the door, the fresh parade of youths,
the new arrivals. Perhaps I should be envious.
Their furnaces of love are still ablaze,
the foaming chargers of the ocean breakers
are still to rear for them for many years while
for me, the waves and beaches come to rest.
Technology rains merchandise each season
and moulds foam rubber pillows for their comfort
beneath their shapes; perhaps I should be envious:
but I remember the feel of attic rooms,
the flavour of water and unpolluted wine,
our very struggle for necessities which
no superfluity can substitute;
and while I still can saunter anywhere
they have run out of space to park their cars.
I pity them as I have pitied no-one,

not even fellow prisoners kicked to death,
a dying sister, a small boy ill with cancer -
they hesitate at the door with a fleeting smile in
the corner of their mouths; their rebellion will last
a year or two; they will admire with passion
the foreign totem poles and try to hold the
collapsing sky with badges, flags and slogans
or they will gallop into nothingness
on steeds of LSD for they're unable
to help themselves, let alone the wretched world;
and they will tire and learn to live with revulsion;
their smiles will stiffen into permanent bulges
of muscle and each morning they will pause
before their garages (like primeval man
with club in hand before his cave) and wonder
which way to turn in search of petrol to quench
their thirst, in search of room to build new roads
between the heaps of ash and hills of rubbish
and where the factory chimneys' smoking forests
are still not dense enough - or where to run
and how to find a spot of land still free
with quiet waters by the edge of lakes which
aren't fouled by stinking carcasses of fish
or where to seek a place within the bowels
of their great cities choked by their own wastes,
a place of cleanliness and sanity
while all around the very earth is dying.

UNE FINE, Armand! I am about to leave.
            Translated from the Hungarian by Thomas Land

Micheal O'Siadhail

GRANTCHESTER MEADOWS

Across Grantchester Meadows May has snowed
cow parsnip, hawthorn, chestnut; a stone's throw
from here the Cam grooves slowly towards King's.
An English heaven: 'My real life began since
I came to Grantchester. I eat strawberries and honey.
A perfectly glorious time. Think only this of me.'

I see you Rupert Brooke blazered, flanelled,
a strolling presence in this albescent funnel
of young summer of picnicking under an oak
with Darwin's granddaughters: 'we used to talk
wearily about art, suicide, the sex problem.'
Übermensch, libido, absinthe, fin de siècle.

A 100 rings in an oak which may have seen
George Herbert brooding by the *Came* or Milton
explaining the ways of God now Galileo's sun
no longer danced attendance on our world. Newton,
did you some midsummer hatch along this path
laws to bring our universe back to earth?

'Certainly I approve of war at any price,
it kills the unnecessary.' Evenings of tennis
and cricket. It's the Aegean 1913:
'My poem is to be about the existence of England.'
Dead before the Dardanelles. A circle closes;
the hawthorn almost in bloom, the oak leafless.

Wars. Disillusion. Certainty a fallen idol,
our daylight turns a dice-dance of potential.
Turmoil of change as an old order dies
into us. Herbert must have known the crux.
Does the slow-leafing oak trust without proof?
I know the ways of learning yet I love.

Ghost Brooke you could be my father's father,
yet I'm your elder. Ride my Aeneas shoulder
as Grantchester blooms a lover's carte-blanche,
another innocence. Do you remember how strange
the fulness of the riddle seemed? *The acorn can't
explain the oak, the oak explains the acorn.*

FREEDOM

Enough was enough. We flew
nets of old certainties,
all that crabbed grammar
of the predictable. Unentangled,
we'd soar to a language
of our own.

Freedom. We sang of freedom
(travel lightly, anything goes)
and somehow became strangers
to each other; like gabblers
at cross purposes, builders
of Babel.

Slowly I relearn a *lingua*,
shared overlays of rule,
lattice of memory and meaning,
our latent images, a tongue
at large in an endlessness
of sentences unsaid.

WHILE YOU ARE TALKING

While you are talking though I seem all ears
forgive me if you notice a stray see-through
look; on tiptoe behind the eyes' frontiers
I am spying, wondering at this mobile you.
Sometimes nurturer, praise-giver to the male,
caresser of failures, mother earth, breakwater
to my vessel, suddenly you'll appear frail -
in my arms I'll cradle you like a daughter.
Now soul pilot and I confess redemptress,
turner of new leaves, reshaper of a history;
then the spirit turns flesh - playful temptress
I untie again ribbons of your mystery.
You shift and travel as only a lover can;
one woman and all things to this one man.

THE OTHER VOICE

You came lean and taut, a barrage of innocence
I remember a bluster of haughtiness hiding a boy
still dazed with childhood hurts, a man tense
with desire; slowly I thawed and rocked you in joy.
You mocked our speck of being; I showed instead
of dust a galaxy whirling in the sunbeam's eye;
you cried at the size of eternity, I hushed and said
aeons count as kisses under a lover's sky.
I want no half-measures. I have made this island
of life our kingdom. Have I stinted your ease
or pleasure? No, how could a woman understand
that men still talk of freedom to go as they please?
My love is your freedom. Do or die or downfall,
it's all or nothing and I have chosen all.

DOORWAY

I'd climbed the engineer's cabin steps, knocked
like a schoolboy: Could I have a word with you?
There he stands in flannels, his navy blue
blazer shining, framed by a door he's blocked.

'I'll give a man a hearing', he says. I back
downwards a little, still trying to glimpse
his face. It's London nineteen-sixty-six.
Whoever he thinks he sees is probably black

or at best a step beneath. And I'm effaced.
I stand under sentence: guilt by motherland,
overseen by some blindness I won't understand.
A degradation: such pride and so much waste.

But I grow older, begin to wonder if he
like Plato's tyrant stared at empty space,
confronting nothing and I was a shadow whose face
had long turned away. I refuse this history.

I'm still climbing to a door, trying to retrace
those steps. Tell me why you're afraid of me?
How lonely the eye in it's majesty. See me.
Hold my gaze. I'm nothing but this naked face.

Micheal O'Siadhail

Hugh McMillan

WHO FARTED IN ROOM XIX?

The Madonnas have gone quite green.
It can't have been the Nuns;
zipped up tight in their white frocks
they are removed from this world by
high feats of tailoring.
Dresses stacked like sails,
they glide an inch above the ground
and their nostrils twitch in the arid room
with aromas from another plane.

It wasn't St Sebastian.
His nose is turned up with the pure
stink of sanctity.
Some Americans have stopped measuring
the stigmata and stare at me.
I shrug. Too much *insalata* my shoulders
seem to say but soon I am alone,
left in no doubt about the place
of flatulence in Devotional Art.

Nevertheless, this eruption
has raised some points.
For with all that greasy food surely
the Saints themselves were prey
to the occasional blast, in which case
is it not a holy act?

Probably the Council of Nicea ruled that
the Apostles did not break wind, poor sods.
But then this room with its squeaky angels
and dapper shepherds hasn't much
to tell us about the real world,
except that Dogma produces good cartoons.

I'm off to the Venetian room,
to see the fat ladies.
Give me pagan influences any time,
the smell of fart as well as flowers.

MARINA

When I surfaced,
bloated with towels, eyes wrung out
and pressed between my palms,
Marina was singing somewhere,
a song about the sea.

Waterlogged,
I could see the lick of oceans
and Marina's cave
damp with tellen,
hung with little combs
made from cuttlefish.
I was dumb but I could feel her fingers
butting through a tangle of hair,
see her breast move in coral.

Years went by.
Continents were drowned,
stars arced and sizzled out.
I said at last
"My ardour for you is such
that I will leave the shallow
world of men."
"Oh, that's nice dear"
she said, replacing the hairdryer,
"Do you want anything on it?"

THE ZOO

A speckled gorge of sky
and the sun parting leaves of cloud
with wide white palms.
There's a torrent of children
beating across the grass,

breaking against the steep sides
of ice cream vans,
scattering at the sight of keepers,
red faced parents
or rockhoppers swimming for their skins.

My son's in the middle,
trailing knuckles along the ground,
telling parrots to shut up,
howling like a timber wolf, trampling his zooburger,
rolling mad eyes at the monkeys.
As I drag him screaming past
the Vietnamese Pot Bellied Pigs,
they draw genteely back.
It seems that plain good manners
got these beasts in stir.

Outside, in the hard heat of the evening,
buses swarm and hoot toward the town.
The animals are recovering from
this display of Darwinism,
and the kids are leaving.
They shouldn't cry.
This brush with sad old nature's
just a taste: the jungle's nearer
than they think.

VETERANS

Sepia: the day in stained glass.
A cat asleep in embers
and the smell of drying coats and hats.

They never talk but through
bevelled windows watch
Winter in the steaming wake of buses,
people flailing, caught

in liquid streets
fishtailing fast
in time. Some intrude,
brush coolly past

the old oak bar,
the pitted skin and dominoes.
And always with ice cold eyes
the old men watch the slowly closing doors.

Hugh McMillan

Imagining A City
Dorothy Porter

Giuseppe de Lampedusa, celebrated for *The Leopard* which charts a culture at a crucial point in its decay, remarked in one of his minor critical pieces that the Vienna of Shakespeare in *Measure for Measure* and the Vienna of Graham Greene in *The Third Man* are oddly similar - both represent the corruption of former ideals, both are pervaded by crime and lust, both are full of spies, women and innocents are isolated and oppressed. Greene was writing in 1949 about an actual city of which he had intimate knowledge; Shakespeare in the early 17th century about a city which we may assume he never visited. All cities have two aspects: the abiding idea of the city as revered and deplored centre of religious, military and political power, and the physical presence of the city in identifiable space and time. But it is as hard to comprehend the city in space and time as it is to ignore it. The city in its second empirical aspect turns out to be as much a function of the imagination as in its first. The similarities between Shakespeare's and Greene's Vienna thus become less surprising. Shakespeare's Vienna comes from reading, and the play of the imagination on that reading, but equally Greene must read Vienna before he can imagine it. And reading is not merely a matter of documentation - it is a question of understanding. Fully imagined cities have probably also been documented, but they have, more significantly, been rendered in ways which accord them continuing life in the thoughts of the people who live in them, the people who come to them, and which provide pretexts for writers and artists.

In 1961 I came to the University of Glasgow from Troon. I didn't know what to expect of the city: it had so far been a place with shops, especially Lewis's which had escalators, an Art Gallery, pantomimes, passable sole and chips in Copeland and Lye's, and a reputation for violence. In autumn, 1961 I went with a group of friends to the Central Hotel to hear Nikolaus Pevsner talking about Victorian architecture. Only one member of our group had previously lived in Glasgow, a couple were English. I guess we were, except in age, not all that unrepresentative: there did not seem to be many real Glaswegians in the audience. Pevsner told us our city was the great Victorian city and I remember thinking how odd all this was. A German expatriate was talking in a fine Victorian building which was designed to accommodate people who did not live in Glasgow, and he was describing it as 'our' city. But it was a place to which most of us could lay no claim at all. Whose city was this great Victorian city? It could not merely belong to a handful of deracinated students and a largely immigrant middle-class.

About five years earlier, two students from Glasgow School of Art are viewing the city from 'a threadbare green hill' somewhere about Sighthill.

Travelling patches of sunlight went from ridge to ridge, making a hump of tenements gleam against the dark towers of the city chambers, silhouetting the cupolas of the Royal Infirmary against the tomb-glittering spine of the Necropolis. 'Glasgow is a magnificent

city,' said McAlpin. 'Why do we hardly ever notice that?' 'Because nobody imagines living there,' said Thaw. McAlpin lit a cigarette and said, 'If you want to explain that I'll certainly listen.'
'Then think of Florence, Paris, London, New York. Nobody visiting them for the first time is a stranger because he's already visited them in paintings, novels, history books and films. But if a city hasn't been used by an artist not even the inhabitants live there imaginatively. What is Glasgow to most of us? A house, the place we work, a football park or golf course, some pubs and connecting streets. That's all. No, I'm wrong, there's also the cinema and the library. And when our imagination needs exercise we use these to visit London, Paris, Rome under the Caesars, the American West at the turn of the century, anywhere but here and now. Imaginatively Glasgow exists as a music-hall song and a few bad novels. That's all we've given to the world outside. It's all we've given to ourselves.'

Alasdair Gray may now regret that he gave these hostages to fortune in *Lanark* in 1981. McAlpin questions the validity of Thaw's analysis and is put down. Extra-fictional complaints about gross overstatement are less easily dismissed. I won't concern myself with the justice of Thaw's sermon but rather with its function. But some imaginative writings about Glasgow which might be adduced to refute Thaw were either ephemeral, like newspaper pieces republished last year by William Donaldson in *The Language of the People: Scots Prose from the Victorian Revival*, or temporarily subterranean, like Catherine Carswell's *Open the Door*: underground native traditions are less likely to be of use to the writer than available European ones. What we are getting from Thaw is not factual comment but the insinuation of Alasdair Gray's aesthetic and an oblique explanation of the kind of novel he is writing. The passage imitates the sections of Joyce's *Portrait of the Artist as a Young Man* where Stephen propounds an aesthetic which is a ground-clearing exercise. Thaw's perception of Glasgow as an unimagined city is necessary as a validation of Alasdair Gray's epic ambitions: the method of *Lanark* is premised on the belief that everything is yet to do.

Nor is the task without its exhilarating side. The problems of living in and writing about an over-imagined city are possibly more inhibiting. Venice is the classic case. As Lewis Mumford says in *The City in History* no other city from the 15th century on has tempted more painters to reproduce its image, till it can only be re-imagined by subverting or violating expectation. Every writer who has visited it has felt the need to write about it and many have recorded their difficulties. Thomas Hardy's *Italian Notebooks* signal his problems in finding a point of purchase on Venice's past:

> The Hall of the Great Council is saturated with Doge-domry. The faces of the Doges pictured on the frieze float out into the air of the room in front of me. 'We know nothing of you,' say these spectres. 'Who may you be, pray?' The draught brushing past these seems like inquiring touches by their cold hands, feeling, feeling like blind people what you are. Yes: here to this visionary place I solidly bring in my person Dorchester and Wessex life; and they may well ask why I do it.

> . . . Yet there is a connection. The bell of the campanile of S. Marco
> strikes the hour, and its sound has exactly that tin-tray timbre given
> out by the bells of Longpuddle and Weatherby, showing that they are
> of precisely the same-proportioned alloy.'

This sounds like victory on a technicality. It seems he finds his individual life
reproved and rejected by the weight of the Venetian experience. On a lighter
note Mary McCarthy speaks in *Venice Observed* about the impossibility of
saying anything new about the city: she thought that her sense of the
gondolas as being like coffins was a fresh observation and then found this in
Byron's *Beppo* - she might also have .thought of Thomas Mann.

Alasdair Gray is liberated from these pressures - he can imagine Glasgow,
or rather Glasgows, and look them in the face. His method enables the
creation of a number of different kinds of city and different perspectives
from which they may be viewed. The central section of *Lanark* gives the city
located in specific space and time, hence culturally determined, in which
Duncan Thaw struggles to define himself, to find his meaning in relation to
his own childhood, his family, his friends, the woman he loves, and the
community he tries, more or less ineffectually, to serve. It is a city which
Thaw, even as a child and adolescent, often looks down upon. Confused and
dissatisfied with his life at Secondary School, Thaw imagines a key which
will transform pain and fear:

> Tonight he came to a piece of waste ground, a hill among tenements
> that had been suburban twenty years earlier. The black shape of it
> curved against the lesser blackness of the sky and the yellow spark of a
> bonfire flickered just under the summit. He left the pallid gaslit street
> and climbed upward, feeling coarse grass against his shoes and
> occasional broken bricks. When he reached the fire it had sunk to a
> few small flames among a heap of charred sticks and rags. He groped
> on the ground till he found some scraps of cardboard and paper and
> added them to the fire with a torn-up handful of withered grass. A
> tall flame shot up and he watched it from outside the brightness it
> cast. He imagined other people arriving one at a time and standing in a
> ring round the firelight. When ten or twelve had assembled they would
> hear a heavy thudding of wings; a black shape would pass overhead
> and land on the hilltop, and the messenger would walk down to them
> bringing the key. The fire burned out and he turned and looked down
> on Glasgow. Nothing solid could be seen, only lights - streetlamps like
> broken necklaces and bracelets of light, neon cinema signs like silver
> and ruby brooches, the ruby, emerald and amber twinkle of traffic
> regulators - all glowing like treasure on the blackness.

In this simulation of dark rites of a mythical pre-city past Thaw gropes
for the key which eludes him in the Glasgow of his present life. This present
is transfigured by the perspective gained upon it, but the transfiguration is
achieved only by a loss of solidity, a blurring of distinctions. Later in the
Unthank sections of the novel the view from on high is explicitly critiqued.
Lanark has just arrived by air in Provan and is consequently full of illusions
about its salubriousness. A morose man explains his error:

'You're in the early stages of a Gulliver complex.' Lanark said coldly, 'I don't understand you.' 'The first recorded aerial survey happened when Lemuel Gulliver, a plain, reasonable man, was allowed to stand on his feet beside the capital of Lilliput. He saw well-cultivated farms surrounding the homes, streets and public buildings of a very busy little people. He was struck by the obvious ingenuity and enterprise of the rulers, the officials and the workmen. It took him two or three months to discover their stupidity, greed, corruption, envy, cruelty.'

A cheerful man demurs, but the view of the morose man prevails: 'Since nearly everyone clings to the cloud-cuckoo view it's lucky one or two of us aren't afraid to look at the state of the sewers.' But it is at street level that Thaw must come to terms with Glasgow and at this level he fails, loses his way and ends up as Lanark in the phantasmagoric city of Unthank. He has occasional sentimental dreams of pursuing a personal path through the city which still connects him to community - "Even when very rich he would walk through these streets with such regularity that folk who lived there would set their clocks by him. He would be a part of their lives." It is not clearly the city's fault that this remains a dream. The city is inimical to his kind of creativity but Thaw's personal inadequacies are neatly pinpointed by his failure to remember Marjory's house and her second name. Idealism has to be buttressed by specificity if it is to have any force. The myth of Unthank is usually described as a futuristic dystopia, yet it also has the curious function of linking Glasgow with past word-cities. The phantasmagoric city is already a feature of Dickens' later fictions, particularly *Bleak House* and *Our Mutual Friend*; and the dislocations of the spatial and temporal sense are, of course, characteristics of the cities of modernism. Alasdair Gray signals the dual function of Unthank during Munro's instruction of Lanark at the Institute:

> You have seen a city and think it in the future, a place to reach by travelling an hour or day or year, but existence is helical and that city could be centuries ahead. And what if it lies in the past? History is full of men who saw cities, and went to them, and found them shrunk to villages or destroyed centuries before or not built yet. And the last sort were the luckiest.'

The dislocations themselves figure the fragility or impossibility of relationships or communities within the city. Lanark and Rima cannot progress from the Institute to Unthank until they agree to go, as it were, in opposite directions and even then they keep coming back to where they began and passing the ghosts of their former selves.

Lanark, then, imagines Glasgow as different cities which are paradoxically all the same city, ultimately destroyed in an apocalyptic conflagration. In its comprehensiveness *Lanark* is an enabling fiction for subsequent Glasgow writers. It is further enabling in being synoptic rather than proleptic: it closes rather than inaugurates a phase. For all the futuristic appearance of Unthank and Provan, the imagination is working with materials of the past: the central Victorian city is the focus of Alasdair Gray's spatial and temporal investigation. The apocalypse itself is a triumph of literariness which refuses to rehearse contemporary anxiety. It is thus fitting that the fiction ends on the hill of the Necropolis, among the streets of the dead.

> In one sense, indeed, the city of the dead is the forerunner, almost the core, of every living city. Urban life spans the historic space between the earliest burial ground for dawn man and the final cemetery, the Necropolis, in which one civilisation after another has met its end. (Lewis Mumford, *The City in History*)

In the first volume of *The Victorian City: Images and Realities*, Steven Marcus has an essay, 'Reading the illegible', on Friedrich Engels' reading of Manchester after a 20-month stay in 1842. Engels particularly remarks how the use of imposing and significant facades effectively separate rich and poor: only by going behind the city's civic face may its full text be read. Here is how Engels concludes his examination of Salford:

> It was here I found a man, who appeared about sixty years of age, living in a cow-shed. He had constructed a sort of chimney for his square-shaped pen, which had no flooring, no plaster on the walls, and no windows. He had brought in a bed, and here he lived, although the rain came through the miserable ruined roof. The man was too old and weak for regular work, and sustained himself by removing dung, etc. with his handcart. Puddles of excrement lay close about his stable.

The old man has become urban detritus and this is also the source of his continuing life. There is not a great distance between this and Alasdair Gray's notion of man as the pie that bakes and eats itself. But the means of separating rich and poor, powerful and powerless, in the city have changed radically in this century. The invention of suburbia supported by blue trains and motor cars worked to protect the professional and managerial classes from too-disturbing proximity to urban degradation. But the *coup de grâce* to the notion of the readable city comes with the development of outer-city schemes: it is no longer necessary to by-pass the others, their existence need scarcely be recognised at all. For why would anyone go to Drumchapel, Easterhouse, Castlemilk and so on unless they lived there or knew someone who did, knew personally that is, the powerless and the dispossessed. It is in the gap between the inner city and this undiscovered territory of the periphery that James Kelman imagines his Glasgow.

James Kelman fictions are not at all tentative, they begin with the utter confidence of wholly new material - it is a confidence he shares with some African and Asian writers, and *A Disaffection* significantly uses Okot p'Bitek's *Song of Lawino*. Kelman's undiscovered continent is not merely spatial; it is also linguistic and the two are intimately related. Alasdair Gray describes his world model as "an industrial-west-of-Scotland *petit bourgeois* one". He adds, rightly I think, "but I didn't think that a disadvantage." Indeed the perspectives he achieves on the city are probably only available to the *petit bourgeois*. Such perspectives would for Kelman involve a kind of mythologising which would erode the authenticity of his versions of urban experience. He must eschew the type of fiction which subordinates his people's speech by putting it in quotation marks, pushing it to the periphery in the same way as its speakers have been decanted and decentralised.

Kelman's Glasgow is a city with no temporal depth, almost no past. For the bus conductor Hines, living in a decaying rented tenement, with a wife praying for the comparative paradise of a Knightswood rather than the exile of 'the District of D', the pressures of the future prohibit a meaningful engagement with the past. "The past and the present have got to be considered. When the immediate past is not only today but also tomorrow. What the fuck. The time things they set you up. 5 years is never to be described as 10 minutes. That would be fucking ridiculous. 5 years is a host of days . . ." Hines fantasises about providing his son with the traditional education which will give him a "potted history of this grey but gold city, a once-mighty bastion of the Imperial Mejisteh son a centre of Worldly Enterprise". But the dream of an heroic past disintegrates into a furious awareness of present helplessness and subservience, one of the fruits of such education. The best Hines can manage in the way of historical depth is a somewhat unconvincing picture of the joys of childhood in Drumchapel. "Even going to school's a laugh, throwing snowballs at the lassies, big fights in the playground, sneaking piles of it into the classroom to leave melting beneath your seat, kidding on you've pished your trousers to see the look on the teacher's face. Great; and always plenty of other kids to play with, it's good, a good place, Drumchapel's a good place."

Patrick Doyle of *A Disaffection* has been given the education that is supposed to get you out of the periphery and into the centre. His increasing disgust with the process traps him in a gap-site, an eternal present of indecision and desire. His predicament is enacted through a series of journeys and visits in a Glasgow that is wholly imagined though scarcely ever described. His education has given him a plenitude of historical, intellectual benchmarks which are, however, unassimilable to his present dislocated existence - they are scarcely even "fragments shored against his ruins" since there are no ruins. His deepest engagement with the city's past is his half-hearted commitment to junior football. He likes being part of a football crowd, but when he goes to see Yoker, he looks down at his shoes and misses the only goal. Doyle lives in a Glasgow tenement, "erected more than a century ago" - it haunts him not with visions of past community but of threat and betrayal: "That outlandish image he kept getting of something like a crowd of masked stormtroopers, shadowy dark figures, who rode slowly ben from the kitchen . . ." The only protection Patrick gets from the Glasgow tenement occurs when he nicks up a close to avoid an encounter with his brother Gavin and his family. And he is afraid even to dwell on ways that Glasgow might be better lest he embraces sentimental, falsifying myth.

> Having a snack bar in the area would be good. Glasgow is very short of snack bars. Why did the Rossis not seize the opportunity and open at the crack of dawn so that the solitaries of the district could arrive for coffee and hot rolls & croissants and salami on rye and maybe a couple of fucking bagels, like they get in all these great wee cafes in New York. Elderly couples meeting for a chat across pots of steaming coffee and hot pancakes with maple syrup! Fucking Mark Twain and Peter Pan territory, Never Never Land, sentimental maudlinity.

Doyle's estrangement from the past of the city is paralleled by his separation from his own childhood of which he has no creative memory.

Here Kelman's confident breach of tradition is peculiarly impressive - a Scottish writer who refuses his hero memories of childhood is quite a turn-up for the books. Doyle's brother reminisces about the earlier exploits of himself and their father - his surprise at Patrick's memory void mimics ours.

> Remember how Jackie used to hand us in a couple of loaves now and again?
> To be honest Gavin I don't really.
> Ye sure?
> Eh . . . my memories of the Vernon Street House just areni as clear as yours. I'm four years younger than you!
> Three-and-a-half, said Nicola.
> Three years and seven months, said Pat.
> Still but I thought you'd have minded Jackie, said Gavin.

Gavin lives in Cadder in an outer-city high-rise block with ludicrously inappropriate verandas. Stained and humiliated from his non-decisions at school (does he give up his job or is he forever stuck at a half-open door?), Patrick seeks refuge with his brother. He goes in his car which throughout figures both his isolation and his guilt: his wavering between giving it up and "acquiring a new motor with plenty of in-car entertainment" is paradigmatic of his vacillations. Once settled with his brother and his mates, he finds that he can still up to a point talk their language, but all the concessions are being made by them - he is not so much included as simply not excluded. What dumps him conclusively back in his gap-site is his misreading of the proper size of carry-out. He buys too much. He knows it but he does it anyway. The journey back from his brother's is an impossible one and is never completed. Waiting for a bus is like trusting that Mr Godot will be along any minute. "The trouble", as Doyle identifies it, "was walking concerns elemental factors." Doyle's self-hatred is confirmed by the rain's assault. He is left in the dark in this no-man's-land between rejecting periphery and rejected centre. The voices he imagines hearing are shouting "we hate ye we fucking hate ye".

A Disaffection is open-ended, yet it seems definitive. The story is not, however, wholly bleak, for the pipes that Patrick has found and painted and tried to play leave open a space within which connections may be possible. "Through whatever it was he was doing he was managing to produce this effect of space, a thing that was spatial." The pipes, Doyle tells his niece and nephew, are "lying right at this very minute in time, this very second in the universe, in my parlour." Doyle himself does not effect the journey back, yet the pipes remain in expectant promise.

James Kelman's Glasgow in A Disaffection is a hard act to follow, it may even prove a hard act for him to follow. Any subsequent fiction which fails to engage with the spatial problems he has identified is in danger of seeming unserious or nostalgic. I should like as a brief coda to propose Frank Kuppner's A Very Quiet Street as a possible way of returning to the spaces of the inner city, and to the city in history without insulting the value of individual contemporary lives. Kuppner's quiet street is West Princes Street, where he was born and where on the 21st December 1908 an 83-year-old spinster, Marion Gilchrist, was battered to death. For this murder Oscar Slater, a German Jew, suffered nearly 19 years of unjust imprisonment.

Slater was eventually released after a ridiculous appeal hearing which refused to acknowledge the extent of the miscarriage of justice. With £6,000 compensation, the price of a life, he retired to Ayr, remarried and lived quietly until his death in 1948. In an artfully unsystematic way Frank Kuppner weaves his investigation of the murder and its attendant personnel, the innocent, confused, the lying and corrupt, with his own personal history and that of Glasgow's streets and buildings. Kuppner is, maybe, the New Historicist of Glasgow, constantly on the lookout for the bizarre connections that give significance to lives, streets and buildings that would otherwise be forgotten because they would be unreadable.

(Presumably a ball might lie there for years unmolested, as their owners grew up into perfect imitation adults (or had they been lost there by other children? What other children? We never saw other children in that garden, whether playing or searching. It was, except for our own brief raiding parties, a childless garden. We seemed to be the only children who even knew that that garden existed.)
I find it slightly curious to consider that this was, presumably, the same back garden that the police looked through carefully, so long before, searching for a murder weapon . . . an auger was found, with a few grey hairs adhering to it. But this had been there for a long while, unnoticed, and it was dismissed as not being relevant to the case. (Too bad for whoever the hairs belonged to. (What might one not have found, slumbering untroubled in other back-gardens in 1908 Glasgow? (Or anywhere else for that matter.) Another fascinating, unrecorded collection. After all, this is human history too.))

Kuppner resurrects the urban tradition of the flâneur for whom the clues to understanding the city are always to hand but always incomplete. The book imitates the procedures of the noticing and imagining walker who lets the city guide him, allows it to map itself on his consciousness: "But what can I do but stumble ahead, speculating extravagantly on the limited material available to me." Inevitably Kuppner finds both racial and class prejudice in his city: Slater himself is only one of the city's baffled victims. The social gulf which allows the trial judge to describe Marion Gilchrist's six-room flat as small has its equally alarming contemporary manifestations.

Kuppner can no more solve the city than he can solve the Gilchrist murder - but the value is in the effort, however fragmentary the result. Marion Gilchrist's life would have passed unrecorded by history had she not been murdered, yet it would have been a life. The secret lives of a city are unimaginably immense and significant. Kuppner struggles to a sense of discovery which is both spatial and temporal. Marion Gilchrist comes to stand for all the other names: "these bookfuls of names which sink further and further from sight; which once were the latest and most up-to-date volume, but fall, despite their impossible variety of life, further and further back on the reference shelves." She is the city's past and our future. And our lives, like hers, are formed out of a web of relationships that we will never perceive let alone comprehend. Kuppner describes this complexity as "the mutual independence of contemporary lives", not a bad way of typifying the archipelactic existence of the city dweller.   Dorothy McMillan (Porter)

Crìsdean Whyte

AS T-EARRACH

Dol am faid aig feasgaran
soillse an-fhoiseil san speur
èirigh uachdaranach an t-sùigh
anns gach craoibh is preas, is dèine
ghineamhainn sna beathaichean,
brodadh geur a' mhiann gan spreigeadh,
dòirtidh mise cuideachd mo shìol dhuit,
a thuathanaich, a bhuanaich gach uile arbhair.

A' TILLEADH BHO BENNETT'S

Baile iongantach na mochthrath
ga thilgeil bhuainn, mar a thilgeas
sinn ar n-aodach, rag le fallas
is smùid, aig ceann dà fhichead mìle,
ri taobh leab' air a dearmad,
iucharlann a' chamhanaich
's meòir na grèin' a' cluiche air
(ach dùinidh sinn na cùirteanan).

Rathad againn ri dhèanamh fhathast
sìnt' an oidhche bhrèig an t-samhraidh,
ùird a' chiùil a' bualadh trom
nam eanchainn, is ìomhaigh chuirp
nach do mhealladh leam san danns'
gam thàladh fhathast, thus' a' cur
cassette a thairgeas tannasg fann
den fhiadhachd rinn ar buaireadh.

Thusa sàmhach aig a' chuibhle,
dùint' an sàcramaid de luaiths,
Alba chadalach mun cuairt oirnn
gun mhothachadh dar ruitearachd,
ach seall! Dhòirt siùga fhuar an là
airgead beò san lochan sin,
dh'ionnsaich e mu theachd na grèin
mun do mhosgladh còs no frìth.

Ghlac meanganan cràidhteach nan dos
cirb chleòc an dorchadais,
thug iad greim an diorrais air,
cha leig iad e mu sgaoil gan deòin.

Illustration to 'Spring' by Gillean Ferguson

Christopher Whyte

SPRING

Evenings getting longer
restless light in the sky
sap rising imperiously
in trees and bushes, urgency
to procreate in animals,
desire's sharp goad egging them on,
I too will spill my seed for you,
husbandman, reaper of every harvest.

COMING BACK FROM BENNETT'S

Astonished dawn city
thrown from us, as we'll throw
clothes stiff with smoke and sweat
beside a neglected bed
forty miles away,
twilight keyboard
the sun's fingers play on
(but we can close the curtains).

A road still to be travelled
stretched in the fake summer night,
music hammers beating heavily
in my brain, the image of a body
I couldn't tempt into the dance
still haunting me, as you put
on a cassette that offers a pale
echo of rhythms that drove us wild.

Silent at the wheel, you're shut
in a sacrament of speed,
Scotland sleeping all around
indifferent to our riotousness,
but look! The cold jug of day
has filled that loch with quicksilver,
it learned of the approaching sun
before the moors or hollows were stirred.

Branches of tormented bushes
have caught the edge of night's cloak,
clutching it to them stubbornly,
they won't be keen to let it go.

Mòr lasadh ann an àird an ear
a' cur nan craobh nan ruaig le maoim,
na stuic crùbte fo eallach throm
prìsealachd na dosraich ùir.

Ciod e nì ar casgadh-ne?
Tha am *motorway* na shaighead
a dh'amais sinn air duaisean
luathghàireach an àm ri teachd,
sinn a' sracadh drochaidean
o bhun nan speur mar chèisean-litreach
gus an rùisgear dhuinn mu dheireadh
sgrìobhadh soilleir briseadh latha.

ALBA, CHI MI A' CHRIOSDAIDHEACHD

Alba, chì mi a' Chrìosdaidheachd
na ceò ag èirigh suas bho do lòintean,
rèidhlean is garbh-shlios a' fuadachadh
na taiseachd thruim a bha cho fad a' lèireadh
cnàmhan na talmhainn, is i ri dàil
na deataich chaointich fhainn air leathadan
gach stùic is slèibh, ach aintighearnas na grèine
samhrachail a' sùghadh suas gach boinne;
glaicean is frògan, tulaichean is cnuic
a' nochdadh ann an soilleireachd ùir-leòis
cho cruaidh gur gann gu fulaing leirsinn e,
dealbh nam mullach àrda dol an gèire,
fèath-nan-eun a' cur a' pheannsail teòma
a dhuibhreachadh nan iomall is nan loidhn',
gun eadhon neul a leigeas sios a sgàil
gu bhith na dhuaichneachd shiùbhlaich air an leirg.
Cha do dh'fhoillsicheadh tu riamh dhomh
cho fìreanta, cho bòidheach no cho lom.
Tha fhios agam nach fhuirich thu mar sin,
gun tig stròdhalachd dhiadhachdan ùr
a-mach nan sìol, a lìonas gach baile,
coille, gleann is cladach. Ach mo dhùthaich,
roghnaich samhlaidhean cho ioma-dhathte,
neònach, caochlaideach, daonnachdail, faoin
's a ghabhar, is gum bitheadh iomlaid
agad ri gach poball a thachras riut.
Gum bitheadh lìonmhorachd a dhiathan agad
air dòigh 's gum faod gach neach a stiùireadair
fhèin fhaighinn, 's gum bi truacantachd na cuid
as lugha na cuidhteachadh do chruadal càch.

A conflagration in the east
sets the trees fleeing in panic,
trunks are bent beneath the heavy
precious load of the new leaves.

Who can put a stop to us now?
The motorway's an arrow loosed
at tomorrow's glorious prizes.
We tear bridges like envelopes
from the backdrop of the sky
until at last the brilliant hand-
writing of day is clear to us.

SCOTLAND, I SEE CHRISTIANITY

Scotland, I see Christianity
lifting off you like a mist,
meadows and rough moors expel
the heavy damp that set earth's bones
aching so long. It hovers, a weak
and mournful fog above the curve
of hills and ridges, but the summer
sun unrelentingly absorbs
each drop. Hollows and crannies, mounds
and knolls stand out in this new light
so clear the eye can hardly bear
to look at them, the summit contours
grow ever sharper, total calm
sets its pencil darkening
outlines and edges. Not one cloud
lets down its shadow to disfigure
a field for a moment. I have never
seen you so true, so lovely or so naked.
I know you won't be that way long. A swarm
of new divinities will emerge
and fill each town, valley, wood
and shore. But my country, choose gods
as multicoloured, strange and changeful,
human, inconsequential as you can,
and barter them with each people you meet.
Have as many gods as possible
so everyone can find the guide they need,
and the mercy of the smaller part
make up for the cruelty of the remainder.

AN FHEARG

An fhearg, an fhearg,
tha 'n fhearg gam cheannsachadh!

Chì mi na boireannach i, na garbh-ruith
tro choille san dorchadas, ach tha a corp
na dhòrn-leus beòthail! Tha an teine
ga bhiadhadh le brìgh, ach 's e a' mhìorbhail
nach caithtear ise leis! Tha a com
geal le neart an losgaidh, teangannan
siùbhlach a' sgaoileadh a-mach air a gàirdeanan
is slos mu cruaichnean, 's a' dol an deirge!

Is cearcall na bàinidh bailbh a beul,
is chaidh a sgreuchail cho fad às 's gu bheil
a ceud sgreuch ga thoirt air ais bhon talamh
is bho na speuran, na ath-fhuaim fheirge mhùchas
na dh'èigheas i a-nis. Cha chluinntear i
aig bodhradh a gutha fhèin.

Tha a' choille dorch mu coinneamh
ach far na deach i seachad, fhuair
na craobhan losgadh bho oir a h-aodaich dheàrrsaich
's chan e sa choill' air cùl
ach crainn ri crathadh an gaoith mhòir
an sgriosa lasraich fhèin.

Tha mi fo iomagain mun t-saoghal
mura thèid a ruith a bhacadh.

COMHRADH AN INNEIL-GHAOITH

Cha bhi mis' a' cur strì dhuit tuilleadh.
Dh'fhalbh mo threòir: aithnichidh mi e.
Thug thu air falbh gach uile nì dhìom
air dòigh 's gum bithinn lomnochd fod làimh.

Air mo roghnachadh 's mo thrusadh,
thug sgian gort do dheuchainn dhomh
cuimireachd an fhiodha strìochdta.
Fhuair mi bho do locradh cràidh
an rèidhe mhìn nach atharraich.

Tha mi neo-ghluasadach mar dhannsair
rag is corrach a dh'fhanas ri
toiseachadh ciùil, is theireadh neach,
's e faicinn deacaireachd mo choir,
gun d' threig gach gluasad nàdurra mi,

ANGER

Anger, anger,
anger is taking me over!

I see it like a woman
running headlong through a wood in darkness,
her body a living torch! The fire
feeds on her essence, but amazingly
it doesn't consume her! Her belly is white
with the strength of the burning, moving tongues
spread out along her arms and down her hips,
growing redder and redder!

Her mouth is an oh of silent rage,
her screeching has travelled so far
that the earth and the sky are sending back
the shout she began with, an echoing anger
that stifles the cries she makes now.
She can't be heard because
her own voice is so deafening.

In front of her the wood is dark
but where she passed, the trees have caught fire
from the edge of her blazing dress,
and behind her there are only
black trunks swaying in the great wind
of their destruction.

What will happen to the world
if nobody stops her?

WHAT THE CHANTER SAID

I can't hold out any longer.
I confess it: I've no strength left.
You took everything away from me
so as to have me bare in your hands.

Chosen and cut
I got from your harsh, testing knife
the shapeliness of yielding wood,
your plane of suffering produced
a regular, smooth finish.

Now I'm frozen, like a dancer,
rigid and unsteady, waiting
for the music to begin: anyone
seeing my awkward pose would think
I couldn't make a natural movement,

gun do thug an t-oilean as mo chom
am faireachdainn 's an t-subailteachd.

Ach nuair a thèid an ribheid gheur
a shàthadh ann am uachdar-sa
's a chuireas tu do bhilean rithe
a' cur mo chom air crith led cheòl,
gam lìonadh le t' anail-sa,
is i co-dhlùthachadh nam bhroinn
an deòir neo-fhaicsinneach de sheile,
tuigear ciallachadh mo phèin,
thèid m' àmhghar na teachdaireachd.

DI-DOMHNAICH SAN FHAOILTEACH

An-fhois na gaoithe
fhathast gun a sàrachadh
fad lathannan na gaillinn sin
a' crathadh dearcagan a' phris,
na bagaidean searbha teann
ag aiseag mo smuaintean a-null
thuige, thar bheàrn nam mìle mìle,
thar fhosgladh leòin a dh' fhairtlich e air m' fhuil
dheirg a dhùnadh le a cruadhachadh,
reubadh na feòla air gach taobh
den sgaraidh sin, ach fuaigheal mall an dòchais,
seòlta, gun fhios, gan caoin-tarraing ri chèile.

DHAIBH-SAN A NI AR LEUGHADH

Faodaidh sibh na sgrìobhadh leinne leughadh
ach cha bhi e riamh nur comas ar n-àgh
a ghlacadh, luathghàireachd an deachdaidh;
ise aig ceann na staidhreach duibh'
san t-seòmar àrd, aig meadhon-oidhch'
a' snaidheadh cunntas air gach gaol,
esan am bothan falaichte
aig bun glinn chumhaing, a' fuasgladh iarna
feallan buaireasach nam manach,
fear eile aig tòiseach dealbha-cluich
gun ach dithis a' còmhradh air cladach lom;
loidhnean ar spuinnidh dol nan lìon
drillseanach bho thaigh gu taigh
càiricht' air na sràidean dorcha,
cruinne-eòlas cruthachaidh
a' mìneachadh nam bailtean dhuinn,
sinn a reub bho shruthadh tìm
gach saothair shoinneant' a dh'fhan nar dèidh.

Christopher Whyte

as if training had robbed my body
of feeling and suppleness.

But when the sharp reed is thrust
into my upper part, and you
put your lips to it, and set
my body trembling with your music,
and your breath fills me, unseen
saliva tears condense inside me,
the meaning of my pain is clear,
my suffering becomes a message.

JANUARY SUNDAY

Restless wind
these days of storm
have not yet tired
shaking the berries on that bush,
tight, bitter clusters
carrying my thoughts across
a thousand mile gap to him,
beyond an open wound my blood
still hasn't sealed with its red crust,
a separation with torn flesh
on either side, but hope slowly
stitching, skilful and unnoticed,
gently drawing them together.

TO THOSE WHO WILL READ US

You can read what we wrote
but you can never grasp the joy,
the exultation in the writing,
she at the top of a dark stair
at midnight in a high room
carving the story of each love,
he in a hidden bothy
deep in a narrow glen, unravelling
the treacherous intrigues of monks,
another just beginning his play
with two men talking on a bare shore,
our current's grid a brilliant mesh
from house to house along dark streets,
geography of creativity
interpreting the cities,
as we tore from flowing time
serene works that outlasted us.

Christopher Whyte

Shanty Town

Sam Gilliland

I watched the little gypsy girl squat and urinate as naturally as any other animal. Dark, sombre eyes scrutinised me as she pished, probing, I think, for the possibility of a few coins; but, as she stood up, a toss of her dark hair and a withering look of defiance indicated that she had decided otherwise.

She looks about twelve years old going on twenty, and is wearing a grimy floral frock that only just reaches her knees. Nothing else. No underclothes, no shoes, no ribbons in her hair and her heart is already turning to stone.

My attention was first drawn to her as she and, I must assume, her sister, walked across the little square between the fish and fruit market. The ground is strewn with sharp stones and there is nothing dainty in her stride. God, I thought, she must have feet like leather. Her sister is wearing little white wellingtons; well, they were white when new. Anyway, the stones don't bother her, and she is carrying the lid of a cardboard box into which they have crammed, as far as I can see, lettuce and cabbage leafs along with a few potatoes and the entrails of fish. The sister pauses only momentarily as 'dark eyes' squats and then moves on in search of other things. For a moment I wondered if I should take her into a shop and buy her shoes. But there are so many other children like her, and anyway, it would almost certainly be construed wrongly, and I get a feeling of helplessness. She turns to look at me before entering the throng of market people again. Little girl, go into your dark future. I have no blessing to give you.

The houses are nothing more than pieces of board nailed together to form a square. Some of them have tin roofs, and others the luxury of corrugated asbestos sheeting which must help cut down the noise of rain during a storm. It was quite hot and one of them had its door open. I was curious, so I looked inside. There is hardly room to turn in there. Certainly not the space for two people to pass by one another, and the walls are blackened with soot. Soot, or the smoke from the one paraffin lamp I see hanging on a wall, for there are other hanging hooks, but they are empty and they must shift it as the wood underneath grows too hot.

I expected squalor, but the interior, if not exactly clean, is neat and tidy. The furniture inside consists of a couple of chairs, a wooden orange box upended with a few garments folded on top, and a table. The table and chairs have been scaled down to suit the place, and there are other smaller items around but it is too dim to make out exactly what they are. The floor is earthen, packed hard, and it looks almost level. There is a brazier just outside the door and my hand tells me that it has been in use that morning, so I wonder if this is where the cooking is done. If so, what about the rain? And where do the occupants sleep? I suspect that there is a door inside that I cannot see, for the building is certainly bigger than this one room, and I am not about to pirate any more of their privacy. Behind the buildings runs a foul smelling canal cum sewer. It is littered with all manner of things and I curse them for not doing something about it.

Further along the row I come upon stone buildings with corrugated asbestos roofs. There are men outside one of them working nets, and a glance tells me that the rest of the stone buildings are used exactly for the same purpose. Nets and other fishing gear stacked outside of them. Across from the buildings towards the sea their boats are drawn up, most of them stelled up with wooden props, and by the look of them some have not put out to sea for a long time. It is easy to imagine that these stone buildings used to house the fishermen's families and that they have moved on to better dwellings. Obviously, some of them still harvest the fish, but further out in the bay I can see larger craft, all with engines, and the real reason for laying up the small boats glares back at the men who stare out to sea and chatter as the nets are being repaired.

At the end of the town, just where the tourist buses disgorge their cargoes, there is a bar, a beer hut. Nothing more than that. A beer hut. There are a few Portuguese fishermen lolling around outside drinking, and two Scots sitting in the only chairs outside the hut. One, a loudmouthed Glaswegian, delighted that he has found a bar that charges only fifty escudos for a glass of brandy.

I am thirsty, so I order a beer. The barman brings the bottle out to me and goes back for a glass. When he returns I already have the bottle at my lips so he shrugs and goes back behind the bar. The beer is a little warm, but good, and I have drunk almost half of it in one go. The Portuguese settle back to their conversations and the loudest Scot calls for more brandy. I watch the barman pour out the two drinks. There is a fair measure in the glasses and he empties the dregs of that bottle into one of them and takes them over to the Scots. He is quietly deferential as he places the brandy on their table and I feel slightly disgusted. I see him bend down behind the bar and pick up another bottle of brandy. The empty bottle is beside him along with a dark brown pitcher. He inserts a little blue plastic funnel in the neck of the empty bottle and decants half the quantity of the full bottle into it then tops up the rest with water from the pitcher. Aware that I am watching him, he looks up. I shrug. After all, we all have a living to make. The Scots cannot see him, and when he straightens up the full bottle of 'brandy' takes its place on the bar. I order another beer and drain what's left in my bottle. The other Portuguese know I have seen the exchange of brandy for water and their conversation is a little subdued as the barman gives me my drink.

"It's free," he murmurs in Portuguese.

"No. Thank you." And I hand him two one hundred escudo notes. "Buy the Scots another drink."

The exchange is in Portuguese and the barman roars with laughter. The fishermen are wondering what the joke is, and the taller of the Scots, aware that they are the butt of the joke, glares at me with suspicion. The barman tells the Portuguese as he fills out a drink for the Scots and the place is a sea of laughter. The Scots are delighted when they realise I have bought them a drink and join in the merriment by ordering the rest of us another. I am the toast of the Portuguese and even the Scots, though they do not understand why. And we are *not* drinking brandy. Yes. This is the place to be.

Sam Gilliland

The Chicken Run

Ann Lingard

Iain sighed in unacknowledged anxiety and anticipation of the climb ahead. The narrow path crept around boulders, across streams and through patches of loose rock and pale rough grass, with no concession to the steepness of the hillside. This was no Victorian stalker's path, built by workers of mountain and moor, but an escape-route, beaten into the ground by people urgent to reach the air and freedom of the ancient hilltops.

Pushing his hands deep into the pockets of his worn grey breeches, Iain resumed his steady plodding, eager now to be separated from the road through the valley. No other car had passed since his family had left him a quarter-hour previously and now, as he entered the wide gully, the air was still, with only the sounds of running water and the occasional sticky squelch of his footsteps on water-logged peat to keep him company.

In these northern hills, spring still lingered and he gave a gentle 'hmph' of pleasure at the patch of short-stalked violets huddling in a hollow. A good omen, surely! Today he would conquer this grey old mountain whose head and shoulders were split by plunging gullies and tiered pinnacles. He had studied the mountain from every possible vantage point since he first saw it two weeks ago; when grey curtains of rain obliterated it or cloud sat surly on its top, he had read his hill-walking guides or studied his map, trying to imagine the obstacles that the ridge would provide. His family teased him about his growing obsession, but instead of shrugging and enjoying the banter, he had become ever more tense, certain that the only purpose of the holiday was to climb that hill. All the rest had just been preparation.

Last night, listening to weather predictions in the pub and on the radio, he had acknowledged that the next day was his last chance. He packed his rucksack carefully, including plasters, a spare bootlace and a torch as well as his usual collection of warm and waterproof clothing; he sought out various treats from the store cupboard, chocolate biscuits, fruitcake, peppermints, and filled his sandwiches with salad and several layers of ham. His daughter suggested that since he was preparing enough food for two, he was actually treating the blonde woman in the bar to a picnic. Lighter-hearted now that the adventure was decided upon, he laughed, telling her instead of a secret grassy hollow behind the mountain where he would spend the day in the company of wild, red-haired women. So amusing was the joke that his children were encouraged to hide rocks in his sack: to 'cramp his style', as the boy remarked without full comprehension to his sister.

In that alert sleep that often precedes a long-anticipated event, Iain dreamt many times that he was walking the mountain: once he slipped, and woke, gasping. Waking with the early dawn, he was convinced that the walk was over and sighed gratefully to think that he could sleep late this morning; with recognition of the dream, came also surprise at his disappointment.

The hillside was solid under his feet, the cloud layer solid too, but high and flat-bottomed, and he looked forward to the view of islands, seas and hills. Gaining height quickly because the path was steep, he glanced often at the expanding landscape behind him. Moving patches of sunlight caught the rocky side of the valley, the quartzite crest of a far ridge, a cottage by a stand of spruce, and brought an answering gleam from the dark waters of the loch. A car stopped on the road below and manoeuvred onto the verge. The movements of the two figures who got out - sitting to haul on boots, standing with heads bent over an outspread sheet of paper - indicated that here were hillwalkers. Usually, when alone on a hill, Iain was aware of his own vulnerability and was pleased to see other walkers, but now his tall body became thin and angular, his beard jutted with hatred and he bellowed (in a harsh whisper, in case they could hear): 'Go away! Get off my hill!'

He turned back to the track; suddenly all the frustrations and anxieties of his daily working life rushed in and engulfed his mind, and he cried out, the long grooves in his cheeks deepening in misery. His stomach clenched and cold nausea swept over him, his head swamped with fragmented memories of uncompleted tasks, unsatisfactory confrontations and faces of old adversaries. 'No, no,' he cried, 'not now! I'm escaping. Go away.' And he stumbled upwards, over the uneven ground, slipping on the broken rock, forcing himself to go faster and faster so that the need to concentrate on the path would obliterate his thoughts. He began to gasp, sweat pouring down his forehead and back; when he stopped, doubled up, to gulp in air, his head was filled with the deep rustle of his rapid heartbeat. The sound steadied him. 'You fool,' he told himself sternly, 'you fucking fool.' He grinned; it was not a word he normally used but he liked the sound of it.

The air darkened as the cloud layer descended and the top of the ridge was hidden. Anger and disappointment had vanished with the expletives, his mind was blank as he picked his way upwards. The two figures below had stopped; one was gesturing at the cloud, the other sitting down. Perhaps they would turn back. 'Huh, fair-weather walkers,' Iain snorted, feeling superior in his sense of purpose. As he clambered around sharp boulders, the soft greyness descended coldly around him and all view and sound was blotted out. As a competent navigator, he was not concerned and, in any case, the ridge must be followed to its end. He no longer regretted the absent view, for now everything was simplified: it was just him and the mountain. Reaching the ridge he was gratified to find the path well-marked and strode easily to the east. The cairn that marked the eastern end loomed out of the mist and, piling on warm clothes, he crouched in its lee to eat a sandwich, fleetingly yearning for sheltered, grassy hollows. It was too cold to delay long, so he retraced his steps and continued west.

The track became rougher as he puffed and scrambled up a steep slope of shattered grey rocks to the top of the first peak. Tiny drops of moisture beaded his hair and beard, and the rock was damp and slippery underfoot. All his attention concentrated on his feet and he delighted in the way his foot or hand moved naturally to places in the rock that had been friction-polished by others before him. He sat deep in a cleft to eat some cake and chocolate, and was surprised to find it was only midday. Were people in the valley below also locked in grey timelessness? Although not religious, he derived some idle amusement in wondering whether he - or they - were topographically nearer to the ultimate Perfection? Of course, it depended on whether you believed in a Heaven 'up there' (in which case he was well up the ladder) or in the transmigration of souls to other animate objects (if so he might be better off in the valley - he hadn't seen even a ptarmigan today). He savagely pushed aside the thought that was needling its way in, that it was other people who were hell, and took refuge in repacking his sack.

A faint track led down across the stony surface and he followed it, his mind still on Nirvana and ptarmigan. Then it seemed to disappear over the lip of a rise and, confident that it would pick its way down the contours, he went on, only to be confronted with a steep drop into nothingness. The track vanished at the very edge. How could he have missed his way? But there was no other track. Suddenly alert, he was certain he heard a car, down below on his right. On his *right?* That was impossible, it was a trackless river valley. Hands clammy, he pulled out his compass and was bewildered to find himself heading south. But the ridge did not go south. Crazy ideas about landslips, even being on the wrong mountain, flashed through his mind. He wrenched at the zip on his rucksack, dragging out the map and tearing its cover in his haste. Finding the hill, he traced its outline, resting the compass on the open fold. He snorted with relief as he saw that a southerly spur - a viewpoint! he snorted again in amused disgust - shouldered out from the peak. In his preoccupation he had failed to take the northern track.

This carelessness had cost him time and he hastened back, a little unnerved by his mistake, to find the junction in the path. Down at the col, among the boulders, the path divided again, as he knew from his reading, and he also knew that despite the cocooning comfort of the cloud, he would not take the upper path along the top of the pinnacles. The lower parallel path was narrow, pressed close to the wall; sheer drops that he could imagine, even though the mist hid them, fell away to the left. He tightened his pack-straps and forced himself to walk calmly. Occasionally, he grasped the rock or rough grass on his right for comfort. His foot dislodged a pebble which clattered down and out of sight and then he skidded on a loose mat of gravel, swaying unbalanced for a moment while his scrabbling fingers tore at and caught the earth wall. Grasping tightly, he swung towards the wall and pressed his head against his shaking arm. 'Fool!' he whispered again. Carefully he let go and stood straight. His fright reverberated in the emptiness of the place. Somewhere behind a small rockfall clattered and slithered. He continued on the twisting path, breathing quickly. On his left the mist swirled to reveal a vertical plunge of hundreds of feet, and the dry grass near his ear hissed in the air current. His skin tingled and as he opened his mouth to gasp, an unearthly howl wavered out into the gloom.

He stopped. Another howl arrowed out, a third. His terror was so great that he became mindless, a fleeing animal moving faster than humanly possible, clawing the side, slipping, but still escaping. Ahead of him, was a gaping hole, the path washed away. An easy jump, a distance jumped for fun by children in a playground but, as the mist thrummed with another sobbing cry, an impossible obstacle. With a moan, he dropped to his knees, slipped off his rucksack and, pulling his hood over his head, curled up in a ball.

'Are you alright?' a quiet, concerned voice asked. The man's eyes seemed to be open but he did not respond. 'Can I help?' the voice asked again. A round, ruddy-cheeked face, hood thrown back from a tangle of dark hair, came into Iain's tiny field of view. A hand touched his arm and held out a thermos cup. 'Would some coffee help? I'm afraid it's not very hot.' Iain stared dully, now past disbelief; he slowly uncurled himself and, wetting his dry lips with the tepid coffee, muttered, 'The howling . . ?'

The heavy eyebrows of the young man puckered and his dark eyes stared searchingly at Iain. Then an expression of understanding and ineffable kindness transformed his face. 'I'm so very sorry. We didn't know anyone was near, we thought you would be miles ahead by now. It was Ruarie.' He gestured above their heads. 'My friend. On the pinnacles. I preferred the safe way. We were joking that this was like a chicken-run - chickens safely cooped up, you see, and the fox pacing dangerously outside. I'm afraid he got carried away. I'm Tom, by the way.' He watched the big bearded man carefully, relieved to see the taut grooved face relaxing, awareness coming back into the eyes. 'It was unforgiveable. We disturbed you.'

'I'm not sure . . . I can't explain . . .' The man pushed his hood back and stiffly stood up. He could not think what to say . . . 'I'm Iain . . . by the way.'

'I seem to have been blocking the pathway,' he commented drily, and he turned his face away as he searched in his rucksack for some fruitcake.

'I'm glad you waited. With my short legs I'd never have got across that hole,' grinned Tom. 'Thank goodness you're here to give me a hand.'

Iain turned to look at him in delight, warmth spreading round his heart. A quiet smile illuminated his haggard features. 'Oh, thank you,' he said.

Shouldering their packs, mumbling through mouthfuls of fruitcake, they both easily leapt the gap, Iain first, offering a token hand to Tom who grasped it lightly. In a few minutes a voice called, 'Hello there, Tom!' out of the mist, and Ruari, perched carelessly on a boulder, grinned down.

'Hi, Ruari. This is Iain. Talk about well-met! Half the path's missing back there and he's so tall he just lay across it and made a bridge.'

The way to the final peak was broad and easy, and breath remained for talk. The two younger men talked animatedly, Tom occasionally drawing their older companion into the conversation. As they came off the last peak, meandering down the springy turf, the cloud thinned gradually until they were out and the valley lay exposed below. Iain trailed behind, over-come with the realisation that people down there were going about their daily lives, unchanged and unaware. He felt sublimely peaceful. No fear could ever be as great, no humiliation as complete, as what he had experienced today; daily worries would be trivial in comparison. But, most important, perfection was not abstract, it was here and attainable, in human kindness.

His foot knocked against an obstacle and, looking down, he wondered what the rock reminded him of. A gale of laughter shook him, he picked up the rock and hurled it to one side. 'The stones,' he tried to explain. 'The blighters, my children - put stones in my sack. I found them when I set off.'

Later, as he unpacked uneaten sandwiches, his son asked him, 'Didn't you meet the wild red-haired women, Dad?'

'No.' The delight welled up again in him. 'But I met a fox and a chicken. And the chicken flapped its wings and turned into an angel.' Ann Lingard

Peter Hughes

LUCIO SESTIO (for Peter Riley)

June trees rock breathless in sap and frill.
Slipstream from an invisible wing brushes
Eyelashes as the stomach grasps the erosive
Stone of the years. Cold space within each name
Untouched by Tuscan sun, wind of sage and thyme
Waving yellows of gorse and broom. The space
Seems inaccessible, neglected for decades
Though tucked beneath the heart's full cistern.
Listen to the drip: leakage from the current
Forming tiny channels which will flood and dissolve
Into the estuary of your remotest breaths.
Among these present branchings, parted foliage
Of the self slits light down towards potential
Buds that you can barely imagine, and offer.

ROMAN STORM

Did you feel earlier on the sonorous
empty weight of brassoed skies?
Phrases slipped inside out like lovers' jumpers,
a circus of sentences under operatic cloud,
another of love's catherine wheels
with neither pin nor post.

Lightning connects distantly
beyond the horizon where parallels meet.

BAPTISM

An uneasy combination of Sardinian wine
and Venus has risen over the petrol station.
Memories of embarkations and night ferries
proceed in some swaying parallel of time,
like the moon's reflection riding the wake
on the crossing back from the honeymoon.

Patterns of suburban shadows stretch away
under the brightness of the Pleiades,
between dark continents of cloud that merge
through the sour intimacy of this sleepless night
in the time it takes to smoke a cigarette.
Somewhere a politician looks up 'bayonetting'
to see if it's spelt with one 't' or two.
Somewhere a priest is studying the results
of the recent municipal elections.

The baby sleeps through the subsequent storm
among prints of elephants and penguins
while lousy bright-eyed dogs over the road
hunch between chained gates and lightning.

On the morning after the boy's birth
the church's grubby windows illuminated two
gas cylinders tucked under the altar, and steps
leading down to a dank, rectangular absence.
When the talk turns to baptism, I see the child
a thousand feet higher - a river flowing through
burnished ironstone pebbles and steep forest.
The River Sangro, twenty-five paces wide,
shallow as water poured over the hands,
where they say wolves still come to drink at night.

THE BROTHER

The next evictions take place tomorrow,
a gas fire eating the dust of summer
between spare blue buds and a reddening grill.
The sister he nursed until death, through months
ridden with disease, unease and priests
finally left the world and flat to the church.
He casts listlessly from the island in the Tiber
watching without quite seeing the varnished quill
lean upstream and edge into a backwater.
A year's gone by and still the odd letter
turns up addressed to no one, August brushing
mass upon mass of fig, nettle and elder.
Every evening he waits for it to get dark
as young tench - the little doctor fish -
amble around the bright, unbaited hook.
On his last morning there he pottered out
in slippers past the church where organist
and bride were tottering into a beautifully rickety
Ode to Joy - where resplendent frescoed angels
gaze and punt befuddled sinners through an
unseen crack in the bricked-up gates of hell.

WORKSHOP

Sometimes you just take a big white clod,
shake it off, hold it up to the air
rotating it deftly, or otherwise.
Sometimes you have to scrape features out
with clogged splitting nails.
Violent hurling to the ground has been known

to release patterns of impact -
spread and tail recalling galaxies.
Hours of pounding can render it
amenable to blending with squirts
of foreign matter, cheesy pastes.
Then there are momentary vacancies
when you breathe all over it, not
noticing its diminution till it's melted,
evaporated and condensed on the windows
obstructing the light, hiding the view.

Peter Hughes

Chris Bendon

HAUNTED AUTUMN

On Sunday, the day of visitations,
there are frequent cars whose drivers stare
as if walking were mad, as in America.

                        Across the valley,
yellow starlights of remote farms no doubt simplify
those of videos, bright beside the dull Welsh dressers;
even here, in Dyfed, TV gives
selfconscious images of the global village.
We'd been looking at slides, those frozen Dutch,
Italian icons of pierced or polished flesh,
the trees of melancholic Friedrich,
a Fragonard whose sky, a decadent, stylised quotation
of what would have been a spiritual dimension,
vied, semi-theatrical, semi-sincere
with the luxury of Psyche, her haughty sisters.

                        Here, now,
in the curfew for jet training flights,
Europe's a yellow ceiling, a corridor of oaks
leading to the ruin of a cursed eighteenth century's
once stately home; which handed its paternalist name
to another, humbler, which still survives,
where orphans cry in play in failing light;
West Wales in a silver age.

Without a watch, I approximate the time.
And turn, the only one on earth to see
these particular leaf-falls beneath a sky
which compels introspection: no church for me
today, or any day, yet I come to the river
as to a sacred place, my dog spotlit by

shafts between these centuries-monumental trees,
owning nothing but what I am: not God,
though not godless, not without
a sense of absurdity, yet purpose,
seeing autumns behind autumn like rings of
a decapitated trunk, a reversed hourglass's
déja vu, within line 8's eternal context.

WHERE IS THAT WONDERLAND
ONLY SEEN THROUGH A FINDER?

Lost. No answer.
Only silence here;
that black box
the moment's funeral,
memorial too when something clicks

and there's your
living room, your lover's face
by biased light revealed and shaped;
there's effort, stress
by magic made
an anteroom to heaven, rainbow chased.

I see Beauty recumbent: rub my eyes -
my wife. See an infant intent on what is not-us
first as an unfocussed bald bawling baby
next with a toddler's sharper senses.
A home that is somehow like a poem
- or museum of
spring and summer evenings
by surprising wildflowers graced.

Even the about-to-be-demolished building
a frame for nature, its bare ribs showing
in sun's patina, glad of recognition.

Here's one of her, black-backed, feeding seagulls
hurling to eternity the body of Christ.
And my longlost daughter on an Autumn path
tiny with distance, unwrinkled apple,
forever just two, and engaging, fully engaged,
turning crisp rust leaves
of God's second album.

There it is - the far off land of Cockaigne;
while all the rest was art and sweat,
the wink in the well, end of the tunnel -
framed by imagined unhappiness, far fetched horizons

short sightedly squinted through the lens of the present
a life of achievements achieved by chance pattern
caught on the sly, hardly trying
since love did the work of simple miracle

a world being born aborted with a button

redeemed again as I leaf through an album,
the crooked family tree

           so green, so green.

FALSE SPRING

A skyline glows,
haloing hills
whose grass, blown rudely,

    lightens, darkens.

Yet another First
    of March, yet it is
    a border-
    line case:

will it rain?

Starlings bunch like iron filings
    to invisible magnetic fields;
everything's held
    in expectation.

And sight's lost its tongue:
try to describe, other than with

    a wave of the arm.

Try to translate
the world's vocabulary:

who would be reading it in Welsh? That

    a soaked phone book,
    directory of the listed
    dead, and canned Harp
    is flung on a grave.

That among the resurrected
national daffs, all lit-
ter is in the English tongue?
Though fragmented snowdrops quiver.
Though *dryw* (look up)
        has briefly flown.

                  Chris Bendon

Leaving the Garden

Janet Caird

"Who is there? I can't see through the sunlight. Ah! It's you, Zillah. What have you brought me? Warm ewe's milk and barley cake? With honey? You're a good child. Come, sit down on the soft sheepskins and talk to me. Why don't the others come as often to see me?"

"I think they're afraid."

"Afraid? How could they be afraid of an old shrivelled woman, the bones showing through her skin? No, no, that's not possible."

"It's because you are so old - and have seen and know so much."

"But you're not afraid?"

"No. I love you. I love you because you are old, the oldest of us all; and because you were here from the beginning; and have all the past locked up inside you."

"You think that is a good thing?"

"Isn't it?"

"It's a burden, a weight. I have known old people who lose the burden, and are left without it and feel only the warm sun, cool water, sweet fruits - and good barley cakes. The burden has slipped from them. Yet I who am the oldest of all still carry it. He said it would be so."

"'He'?"

"The voice, the other one; the adversary. No, not that. The partner? But why was I chosen? Or did I choose myself? You see, that is the burden - always there - the question, the 'why?'. But that is no reason why they should be afraid of me. Give me your hands. Look in my eyes. Be truthful. Are you sure it is not hatred the others feel? And blame and condemnation? Why do you turn your head away? Tell me the truth."

"Perhaps some are like that. Not all. The thing is done; we are here."

"He never ceased to blame me. Not openly, but he never lost the dumb sorrow that fell on him."

"'He'?"

"You know, the man . . . This milk is good; and the barley cake . . ."

"Grandmother?"

". . . What? Oh, it's you, Zillah. Did I fall asleep?"

"Only for a little while."

"It happens often now. And for a little the burden isn't there . . . How bright the sunlight is beyond the tent! And the heat - I can feel it creeping in here."

"Shall I fan you with this green branch?"

"No. I like the warmth and stillness. It reminds me . . ."

"Of what?"

"Of that time; those years ago. Before . . ."

"Before what?"

"Oh you know. Everyone knows. Don't pretend not to. The man told you, didn't he?"

"But you never told anyone, Grandmother. I'd like to hear it from you."

"But why? He told it - as he believed it happened."

"But did it happen just like that . . . ? Grandmother?"

"Help me move over to the entrance there. Put the rugs in the shade, where I can look out to the sunshine, and then bring me something more to drink. But this time it must be a cup of wine. Oh yes, I know you others drink wine, but think ewe's milk better for the old woman! You bring me a cup of wine, and sit by me and I'll tell you how it was. Give me your hand. I can't rise easily now. Pile the rugs deep, there by the curtain. Yes, that's good. How bright it is outside! I haven't been out of the tent for a long time."

"I've brought a jar of wine. We can share it."

"Good. Pour me some. Ah yes, it's good. One of the gifts. Have you found a rug for yourself?"

"Yes I have."

" . . .Well?"

"Well what?"

"You were going to tell me how it was."

"Did I say so? But now that you have brought the wine, perhaps I have changed my mind."

"That's unkind. It's - it's wicked!"

"Aha! So you know what is wicked, do you? An old woman tricking you into giving her wine and then refusing to tell you her story is wicked!"

"Breaking your promise is."

"How do you know it is?"

"I - everyone - it just is. You know it is."

"Yes, I know. Who better? I'll tell you how it was. Where shall I begin?"

"The garden; the beautiful garden."

"To begin with, Zillah, tell me what you know of the garden."

"It was very beautiful; and there were trees and flowers and friendly animals; and the seasons passed peaceably; and there were no storms or drought or tempest or earthquakes. There were clear streams and cool lakes and birds of every size and colour and everything was perfect and lovely and there was no fighting or death - until . . . until . . ."

"Until I spoiled it all? That's what they say isn't it? Oh don't hang your head. I know, and in a way it's true. But not in the simple way you have heard it . . . Give me some more wine . . .

"You think - you all think - life in the garden was perfect. the man thought so. He would spend hours, days, just looking at the garden and the beasts - and then he'd make up songs about them. And at night he'd sit under the stars looking and counting and naming them. He always knew his own name but he didn't tell me it, and I was just 'woman' to him. He was completely happy with me and the garden and all that was there. But I . . ."

"You were not happy?"

"Yes, yes, but the difference was that he accepted it all without question. But sometimes waking beside him in the night I would ask myself 'Why? Why are we here?' Once I asked him and he looked puzzled and said, 'We are here. What do you mean by "why?"' so I never asked him again. Then one day he came to me excited and puzzled and told me he'd found a Tree quite different from all the others - so different that it puzzled him. He took me to see it. It was a small tree and it was bearing fruit. Now, all the other fruit-trees were wonders, with fruit that glowed - orange, yellow, purple, scarlet, glossy black, shining white. The fruit of this tree was small and green and round, almost hidden by the leaves. Small, pointed leaves that turned and whispered even when there was no wind. I said, 'Why did you bring me to see this? It is a small, dull tree.' And he said, 'Yes, but it is special. The Voice' (this was a voice that spoke to him in the Garden, but which I did not hear - then -) 'the Voice says we must never eat its fruit.' I said, 'I don't want to eat. The fruits are small and green and unpleasing.'"

"But you did eat."

"Yes, Zillah, I ate it. You know the story. There was no need to eat of the Tree. We had all the fruits of the garden to choose from. The man thought no more of the Tree - but sometimes I would go and look at it and listen to the rustling leaves, and I began to wonder 'Why?' - why had the Voice singled out this small and unattractive tree as forbidden? What was special about it? The man said it was special *because* it was forbidden and he didn't understand the question when I asked 'Why?'. It was simple for him. The Tree was part of the Garden and it was forbidden and that was how things were. But I went on wondering 'Why?', and when he was away looking at trees or animals and making up his poems or thinking out names for things - he was good at that - I would go and look at the Tree and wonder, but had no desire to eat, the fruit was so small and green."

"But I thought the serpent tempted you . . ."

"Oh, that was the man's explanation. He never quite understood what happened. He could not believe I did it of my own free will. So he blamed the serpent. He never really liked snakes anyway. But the serpent was in me, in my mind. Oh it's all too difficult to explain."

"Give me the cup. There's more wine. Drink it."

"Yes, it is good. There was no wine in the Garden . . . What was I saying?"

"That there was no serpent."

"Oh yes. It came to a point when I would spend all the time when he was busy in the Garden just sitting by the Tree and looking and wondering 'Why?' and then one day when I was there and thinking as always by then 'Why not eat?', for the first time I heard the Voice . . ."

"Grandmother? Are you asleep again?"

"No. I was thinking about that first time; of the terror. I couldn't move. I didn't know where the Voice was. Not in the tree; it was nowhere and every-where. Inside me and not inside me. Everywhere, like the air or the light. I was afraid. When the man spoke of the Voice, he never said he was afraid."

"Why were you afraid?"

"It came suddenly; it echoed my thought."

"That was why it frightened you?"

"Yes - no - I don't know."

"What did it say? Or don't you want to tell me?"

"It said, 'You are always asking "Why?". Are you not content to be here like the man, who is Adam for so I named him, for no other reason than that he is here to tend my garden? That is not sufficient reason?' And then there was no voice but only a silence that pressed and pressed on me waiting for my answer. And I had to whisper - I couldn't not whisper - 'No it is not sufficient. Why am I here?'

"And the Voice came again. 'Is it enough to say you're here to help him?'

"I whispered again, 'No. Why is he here? Why is the Garden here?'

"And the Voice said, 'Because I willed it to be.'

"Then it went away as it came; it was there and then it was not there.

"I did not tell Adam I had heard the Voice. I did not tell him that now I knew he had a name. But he saw something was troubling me and asked me what was wrong. And I said I was still wondering 'Why?'. He didn't understand but said I must come with him to tend the Garden and stop being alone so much and sitting by the Tree."

"And did you? Tend the Garden with him?"

"Yes, but I never had the pleasure in it he had. It was all delight to him - every flower, bush, tree, beast, fish, insect - they were all a delight and a wonder to him. If he found a new creature he would touch and exclaim and ponder how to name it. I cannot tell you, you cannot imagine - how wonderful the Garden was. And so much to find out - surprise under every leaf, amazement in every corner. Oh there was richness there to satisfy all the curiosity in the world - except mine and my 'Why?'."

"And because of that it was all lost?"

"Yes."

"I think I'd have liked the Garden. I think I w'd have forgotten 'Why?'."

"I couldn't forget. Adam thought I had forgotten, but I hadn't. And one day when we were gathering glowing fruit from a shrub near the Tree I burst out and shouted, 'Why not from that tree? Is the fruit not good for food?'

"And the cheerfulness went from Adam and he said slowly, 'The Voice said if we eat that fruit we shall have knowledge of good and evil, and such knowledge is not for us. So the fruit of the Tree is forbidden to us.'

"And I said, 'What is this good and this evil?' For we did not know. Can you imagine it, Zillah? We did not know good or evil?"

"The Garden was good."

"But we did not know it was. We were innocent. The Garden was as it was; that was how things were. We did not know we were blessed in Paradise."

"If you had known?"

"Would we have left? But you see, we could not know until we had done the deed that meant we could not stay . . ."

"Tell me how it happened."

"One day I did not go with him to tend the Garden. He was looking for little animals - the insects, the creepie-crawlies. Instead I went to sit by the Tree; the fruits were scarcely visible among the leaves. And I heard the Voice: 'Are you still asking "Why?"?' And I raised my head and said 'Yes'. And the Voice said, 'And what is your "Why?" about this time?'

"'Why is it forbidden to eat this fruit?'

"'What did Adam tell you?'

"'He said you said we should know good and evil if we ate.'

Illustration to 'Leaving the Garden' by Liz Tainsh

"'And . . . ?'

"'Why must we not know good and evil? I want to know. He finds everything he needs here in the Garden. I think there is something outside - beyond - not here. There is you, the Voice.'

"'But haven't I willed everything for you here? Do you lack anything?'

"'Yes,' (Oh, I was bold, I was brazen; I looked back in amazement) 'an answer to "Why?"'

"'You think if you eat this fruit you will have an answer? You think knowing good and evil will answer "Why?"? It will give thousands more "why?"s to ask. and you will have to leave the Garden. No, don't ask "Why?". It is so.'

"The Voice was very deep and stern and I was abashed. So in a whisper I asked, 'Is it only we who are forbidden the fruit? What of the animals?'

"And the Voice said - as if through a smile - 'They do not even see the Tree. The serpent coiled in sleep by the root doesn't know the tree is there.'

"And I - Oh, the arrogance! - said, 'This knowing good and evil. It is a great thing?'

"I told you, Zillah, we knew nothing at all about it; otherwise I should not have said anything so stupid.

"And the Voice changed again and said slowly, 'The biggest thing there is to know and the most dangerous and burdensome.'

"'Is that why you withhold it from us?'

"The Voice didn't answer; for a long time there was silence, but not the silence of absence. And then it said slowly: 'I am not withholding it, I am giving you the choice. I have never given any creature choice before.'

"'Why now, to us?'

"'Your "Why?"s are too many. I should have left Adam alone in the Garden. My beautiful Garden. Is it not a wonder? When you, foolish woman, are not brooding over your "Why?"s, you must admit it is a wonder.'

"'It is, it is. Why are you giving us the choice now to know what is beyond the Garden? I knew there was something beyond.'

"'That is not for you to know. You want to know everything, but you will never know the loneliness of perfection, the wearisomeness of omniscience. You have the choice, to eat the fruit or not, but if you eat you also choose a great and terrible burden.'

"So I was warned. But I didn't understand the warning. How could I in my innocence? That I should have to leave the Garden I saw as a consequence of taking the fruit, not as a punishment. I felt a sense of anticipation and excitement. Now I see it all as part of the paradox - I could not come to a knowledge of good without first doing a wrong - though I did not know it was a wrong."

"We always thought it was very simple. You disobeyed, made Adam disobey, were expelled."

"Things are seldom as simple as that. The Voice is a great complicator at times."

"But you did eat."

"Oh, Zillah, yes. Yes, I ate. I stretched up into the quivering leaves and picked a little green fruit, and ate."

". . . Grandmother?"

"Ah, yes, what happened. At first, nothing at all. Silence, a deep, full silence; everything was still. Then there was a rush of wind that sent the branches of every tree tossing and twisting and tore off the twigs and flattened the grass and the flowers and left them bruised. That was the first result - the Garden was damaged. And I stood there chewing the hard flesh of the little green fruit, forcing myself not to spit it out for it was sour and bitter and hard to swallow. There was no sudden revelation, no blinding light of understanding, only a new feeling, and that was sadness, which I had not known before but which swept over me as I saw the battered Garden."

"Were you sorry you had eaten?"

"I didn't yet know what 'sorry' was. Sad - I know now I was feeling sadness - at the damage to the Garden, but also I knew - yes, dimly, but I knew, oh, it's hard to tell - I knew that now I was more - more real. That I had moved into a world beyond, greater, fuller than the Garden. After the storm of wind, I heard the Voice.

"'Well? Are you satisfied? Has your "Why?" been answered?'

"'No. Not yet. It will be.'

"'That? Never. But you will find many more "Why?"s to ask. You must leave the Garden.'

"'I know. I could not stay. It - it isn't enough.'

"'So? The Garden isn't enough? Do you know what is outside? No of course you don't. I tell you, you will long time and again for the shelter of the Garden.'

"'Why did you let me do it then?'

"'You see? Another "Why?". I left you to choose. You have chosen to leave the Garden. You don't know - yet - but you have chosen to be unique, different from all other creation: not the ruler of my other creatures, but a seeker of reality - Me.'

"And then the Voice went."

"And you?"

"I went on nibbling the bitter fruit. And then Adam came racing through the trees, alarmed, wondering, amazed by the storm. And found me swallowing the last morsel. And he was aghast.

"'We were told never to eat. The Voice said so. Was that why there was the storm?'

"'Yes.'

"'What made you do it? Something must have made you do it. You would never do it by yourself. I know,' he saw the serpent, wakened by the storm, coiling and uncoiling its beautiful, scaly body, 'that thing made you do it. He made you do it. Didn't he?'

"'No, Adam. He doesn't even see the Tree. Only you and I do.'

"'How do you know?'

"'The Voice told me.'

"'You hear the voice?'

"'Yes, sometimes.'

"'Well, then, the Voice must have told you not to eat.'

"'The Voice said I could choose. And I chose.'

"'You plucked the fruit and ate?'

"'Yes.'

"'And its taste?'

"'Was sharp and bitter. And having eaten, I must leave the Garden.'

"'Leave the Garden?'

"'The Voice said so.'

"'Yet you ate? You want to leave the Garden? You want to leave me?'

"I couldn't answer. Because, Zillah, when the Voice said I must leave the Garden if I ate, I had not thought of Adam. I had - yes I had - for the moment forgotten him. But now I saw I must go alone - for he had not eaten the forbidden fruit. So I stood there silent. And then the Voice came.

"'Yes Adam, she must leave the Garden, But you have not eaten. You will stay.'

"'Without her? No.'

"'Ah. Now we are disobedient. This eating of the fruit works fast. You cannot leave the Garden unless you eat too. You have the choice. Eat and leave the Garden with her, or stay alone. You were alone before she came. You had all the Garden for yourself. don't you remember your joy in it?'

"'Yes, yes.'

"'Could you leave all this? Who will tend the broken trees and plants?' "Adam looked at me and looked around the torn branches; and said nothing. But I knew what was in his mind. So I said 'Stay in the Garden.' and he said 'Without you?'

"'Without me. You were here without me before. You had dominion over everything.'

"'But I was alone. Oh yes, I remember. After sunset, watching the stars come out, thinking of the names I had given the creatures that day. And no-one to tell them to. The hedgehogs and tigers, the bush-babies and buffaloes - I could go among them and touch them - well, not the hedgehog - kneel by them and be reflected in their big deep eyes - and tell them their names - and it meant nothing to them. If I had named the tiniest shrew 'crocodile' or the elephant 'hamster' it would have meant nothing to them, though I took such care in the naming of them. Didn't I?'

"'You did, you did.'

"For I remembered how he used to come at night and tell me of the naming. Once or twice he asked me for a name - like the time he brought a little insect, bright gold and green, and said, 'I can't think of a name.' And I said, 'You must call it a "beetle", for that is an absurd name, and it is so beautiful and jewel-like that you could never find a name to suit it. So you must call it "beetle".' And he did. All this went through my mind as we stood by the Tree. And for the first time I knew how I had wounded him. and the Voice said, 'You see? You did not think of him.' And I wept."

"That was the first time you felt tears?"

"Yes, Zillah. The first time. I didn't know what was happening and Adam touched my cheek and said, 'What is this wetness?' And the voice said, 'These are tears. You did not know or need them before.' Adam said, 'I must eat the fruit too.' I said, 'No, no! It is too bitter.' He said, 'Then I will share the bitterness.' He stretched his hand to the tree but the Voice said, 'Adam, why do you want to eat? Do you want to have the knowledge of good and evil?' And Adam said, 'I don't want to be alone without her.' And the voice said, 'I knew it was taking a risk to create her. And now look what's happening: disobedience, rebellion, and not even for a good reason! Another helpmeet could be contrived, Adam.'

"When I heard the voice say this, a new feeling seized me - a mixture of anger and fear and I couldn't breathe until I heard Adam say, 'No, I want Eve.' That was when I knew he had given me a name too, besides 'woman'."

"Was the Voice angry?"

"No, Zillah. That was the strange thing. More resigned. Even - but that couldn't have been the case - as if there were a smile behind it. But at last it was very solemn - very slow and weighty. 'Think, Adam. The Garden is yours now. Once you eat, it is gone from you.'

"Adam said, 'I will go where she goes.' And he put out his hand and plucked a fruit - a little round hard fruit - and bit into it. You know the rest."

"You had to leave the Garden straight away?"

"Yes."

"And out of the Garden you looked back and there was an angel with a fiery sword to keep you out . . ."

"No angel. That was another of Adam's imaginings - like saying the snake made me eat the fruit. He always tried to wrap up unhappy events in a story. When we turned round, the Garden was on fire. I don't know how it happened. But the horizon was alight, and the animals, the poor bewildered animals were driven out by the flames. It was hard for them and they were ever after distrustful of us. That's how it was. You know the story."

"Adam, you say, left the Garden because of you, because he did not want to leave you. And yet, he held you to blame?"

"Yes, that's how it was. He chose to leave because of me, and then bore a grudge because he had - and he accused the serpent of being the cause. Outside the simplicity of the Garden he found things bewildering. He felt the loss more than I did. I had to bear children and rear them and try to comfort Adam and had less time for regrets - even less time for asking "Why?", until I was alone."

"Did you ever find an answer to the "Why?"s?"

"Only half-answers. After we left the Garden I only heard the Voice once, after Adam died. It said, 'Have you found an answer to your "Why?"'

"And I - still proud, still brazen - said 'No, but in time I will.' And the Voice said, 'Beyond time; not in time.' I have never heard it since, and I have never stopped asking. Sometimes, lying alone in the shadows at the back of the tent, I think back to the Garden and wonder. I ate of the Tree of the knowledge of good and evil. So, if I had not been arrogant and rebellious and had not bitten into that bitter little fruit, would we ever have known good? They say only that I brought the knowledge of evil . . .

"Now help me move to the back of the tent. I'll have my usual afternoon sleep. Perhaps, this time, at last I will slip out of time, and the "Why?" and the burden will trouble me no more."

Janet Caird

Donny O'Rourke

FROM THIS AMERICAN VERANDA

This is my first night in the zone of muffins
and weatherboarding - upstate New York: I loaf on their porch

with fireflies, jiggling whisky my uncle's too ill to savour
alone with bougainvillea and the ghost whoops of warriors

along the banks of the Mohawk River.
Inside my uncle plays videotapes of A.L.F., fingers

the tartan tie he asked for . . . "Those MacGregors, boy" -
his liver cancer's inoperable, the night smells not of blossom

but of ground beef and cigars. It's late. I rock and jiggle, rock.
To be one of the first ashore at Omaha. From this

American veranda I see a blacked out Clyde, troopships
in Atlantic mufti, the end of an embarkation leave

a girl in taffeta and tears, a dime store ring
on the finger of a GI bride.

THE DONEGAL DYNAMITERS

Sure I'll have a jar with you says Packie
For didn't I damn near build yon Hydro Dam
At Cruachan meself - a powerful dram
Ye get in Scotland. Mind its fierce tricky
Work dynamiting mountains though I was
On the shovelling side meself - rare town
Glasgow, ye'll know the Gorbals; I lodged in Crown
Street with a Jewish widow's in-laws -
Sound's Irish I know but there you are.
Did ye ever hear o Paddy Crerand?
Well he's a Donegal fella and
So was Patrick Magill, wrote a quare
Wheen about the Navvies so he did. Gave us pride.
A glow? That's just searchlights in the air -
No shortage of dynamiters over there.
Though these days, mostly on the shovelling side . . .

AN EARLY BATH

To prove, I think, despite all evidence
That last night, our first night
Was no mistake, you draw a bath for us
In the first light of this citrus sharp
Spring morning. You wash my hair-oil
My joints with a slow erotic thoroughness -
All this to the sound of Mozart clarinets.

With the tang of your keen astringent
Kisses still sudsy on my lips,
I embrace anew the end in these beginnings

That leave me perfumed and anointed, barely salved . . .

While I brew coffee you soak on
Ticking off on spotless toes the splashy plans
That count me safely in; Dear Geisha,

I'll towel you now, but who will dry your tears?

I have never been so clean or felt so dirty.

ANGUS IN HIS 80S

In this peaty, puddled land
his spade's excalibur;
at eighty-six, still claiming crop
from gale and sucking bog.
The Atlantic's a skiff away -
blue black as plums:
with hair like spume
and in gansey and denims,
he's a fierce tide going out.

THE BEACH AT MAGILLIGAN

That yolky beach, the longest in Ireland
my mother trod in her Northern girlhood.

Now wire and watchtower skulk where she stood
guard over sandcastles: Magilligan Strand

where, behind a steel stockade, searchlights
comb the cells of Nissan hut anchorites.

Donny O'Rourke

REVIEWS

ISLANDS & TENEMENTS - NEW FICTION

That Rubens Guy: Stories from a Glasgow Tenement, John McGill, Mainstream, £9.95; *The Dream*, Iain Crichton Smith, Macmillan, £12.95; *Selected Stories*, Iain Crichton Smith, Carcanet, £12.95; *The Other McCoy*, Brian McCabe, Mainstream, £11.95.

That Rubens Guy, a first novel from an exiled Glaswegian, saves itself from cliché at every turn by its professional approach to its subject. In the years since *Lanark*, the working-class Glasgow of the fifties has been very much with us in fiction. Like Gray, McGill succeeds in presenting a past from which nostalgia is largely expurgated; also like Gray, he creates the necessary emotional distance by his ironic narrative technique. The methods he uses are very much his own, yet part of a long Scottish novel tradition.

The characters who inhabit No 30 are surreal, life-like but larger than life, recognisable but also over the top. This simultaneous reduction and exaggeration makes for a very Scottish kind of irony, making it possible to approach such dangerous subjects as childhood without sentimentality. Some of the strongest scenes centre upon the boys, Wee Pete, Sniffer, Keeking Thomas, John. 'The Stinky Ocean' is terrifying in its acceptance of Sniffer and Wee Pete's single-minded instinct for self-preservation. Idealism vanishes under the mud. Blackmail, not remorse, is the final note. In a very different scene, John's love for the cowgirl Annie McGinty ends with another kind of brutality, and a shadow of something harder, left hanging like a question-mark over John's as-yet-undaunted heroine. The tale from which the book takes its name, 'Baroque', shows Wee Pete as pathetic, grotesque and sublimely honest. He is thrown out of the art gallery for masturbating in front of his favourite Rubens: "I'm barred for ever. The bastit said I swore at them lassies and I didnae. I was just looking at the fucking photies. Fucking Rubens."

Pathos and humour blend well under a skilful hand; the scenes with Big Jessie and Young Jessica in 'The Three Brass Budgies' and 'Pleasure' are hilarious, and the pathos behind the farce is salted with enough cynicism to make it acceptable. If any characters are the victims of reductive sentiment it is the women. Big Jessie is a closer than is comfortable to the whore with the heart of gold. Mina's destructive attachment to Tony and consumer durables is too obvious, embittered Lily Simpson has a soft spot somewhere, and sure enough Tam Burke finds it.

Structurally the book pleases. The episodes stand as separate stories, welded into a novel by a progressive concern for the main characters, and by a sense of the tenement having its own life of which all these lives are part. In fact the tenement and the novel stand as images for one another. Each absorbs and contains the different events and people which give the book its rich diversity. A satisfying parallel, and McGill makes it work.

The Dream, also set in Glasgow, is totally unlike McGill's novel, so firmly contained within its tenement. Crichton Smith is dealing with the Dream, the hopeless yearning for somewhere else, in this case the island which the characters have left, which represents the irretrievable Gaelic past. Again, it is the astringency one admires. Martin, looking back to Raws, is treated by his author with complete respect, but there is no space for sentimentality here. Both author and reader know the dream is only dream, but it cannot be cynically dismissed because it is also real. It is not the island as it is now, nor the exiles as they are now, but it represents something much harder to cope with than mere illusion.

The issue is language. Martin lectures in Gaelic in Glasgow, and his internal crisis is that of a teacher of a dead language living among those who do not speak it. He dreams of returning to Raws and teaching, not as a scholar, but as a speaker of a living tongue. His wife Jean left Raws after an appalling childhood, and refuses to speak Gaelic or to return. Their first meeting is recalled in terms of the power struggle over speech: "To speak, to be forced to speak, if someone speaks to you. She hadn't really wanted to speak to him, but had been compelled to do so."

The couple repeatedly engage in dialogue, or rather, alternate monologue, in which they simply fail to communicate. The question is whether they will succeed in bridging the gap between them in time, to sit down at "the bare negotiating table of reality", and redeem their marriage. As far as action goes, this is really all we have, a small sop to those looking for a story. Instead we are offered a psychological struggle, and a debate on the nature of language, perception and reality. For a novel to sustain this, the characters alone must be strong enough to hold us to the theme.

The epidemic dilemma is: how do two people communicate who inhabit different worlds? Jean's way out leads her outward, she works in a travel agency, fascinated by the possibilities of a wider world. Martin's absorption with the past (his view of it turns out to be as distorted as hers) appals her. Other characters merely act as chorus, often parodying their tendencies. The macabre party of divorced women playing darts on their husbands' photos, the maudlin nostalgia of the exiled islanders, even Gloria with her illusions about a cleaner, freer country, do little more than echo the duet of Martin and Joan.

The book emerges as a study of attempted dialogue rather than a novel - strophe and antistrophe. It works as a novel becaus we become involved with the speakers. There may not be much plot, but Martin and Jean are more than mere voice. They have real parts to play, and Crichton Smith sees that we care how they do it.

Also by Smith, Selected Stories, is a collection, chosen by Smith, of what he considers his best stories. Some are drawn from earlier collections, others are in book form for the first time: it would have been good to have the stories dated.

Crichton Smith has perhaps done more to maintain the importance of the short story in Scotland than any recent single author, and yet one of the first things one notices about his stories is that they have been written by a poet. They are none the worse for that, and here he seems to have picked up on his own poetic quality. There is an intensity of language, a compression of experience into few words, that one more often associates with poetry than prose: "She dragged Paul along like a chain behind her: he clanked in the hot day of her mind" ('The Arena')

And he clutched firmly at his watch, that round golden globe on which he depended, in its exactitude. Always ticking like his heart. Except that unlike his heart it was renewable. ('A Night with Kant')

The stories, like good poems, are ambiguous, teasing, presenting us with various worlds, but offering no more neat conclusions than life itself. Perhaps the hallmark of a thoroughly competent writer is that there is no longer any desire to explain. "The Scream" has a more obvious question attached to it than most stories, indeed the last word makes the question explicit. More often we are supplied with no more questions than answers. In "Napoleon and I", the narrator deliberately solves her problem by changing the way she sees things; up until that point we were led to believe that she was describing a delusion, because that is what it looks like from the outside. She beckons us in. In stories like "The Maze", we begin, as it were, on the inside.

The focus is intensely on individual experience: extraneous matter is pared down to nothing. 'The Survivor' tells us all that journ-alism does not, and almost nothing that it does; not what is happening, but what is experienced. This and another story about violence, 'On the Train', are frighteningly true to that sense of the unreal actually happening that violence seems to induce. Reading these stories is like watching a form of

mental surgery. There is something alarmingly practical about finding words for what is (or appears to be) actually being felt. Perhaps this is all part of the illusion; Smith makes us believe he is bringing us close to what life is really like, by the sheer art with which he tells a good story.

Brian McCabe's first novel, The Other McCoy, also concerns itself with the problematic question of a reality beyond appearance. McCoy is a down and out impersonator, on whom Edinburgh characteristically turns its back. The word play of the title is carried through the book, as McCoy struggles to discover who, or perhaps which, he really is. The action takes place within the day leading up to Hogmanay, and behind the apparently aimless wanderings of McCoy, McCabe works within a carefully-knit structure, almost Aristotelian in its conventions of time and place.

The merit lies in the imaginative exploitation of the identity theme. Language becomes a game, conversations a sequence of riddles and word games. Throughout the novel McCabe the poet is evident in use of language and allusion.

The most serious limitation of the book is perhaps McCoy himself; "not another alcoholic male identity crisis in a corner of a Scottish city", is one's first reaction. The theme has been rescued from banality more than once in recent years, but might it eventually become as hackneyed as any kailyard? McCoy emerges, but only by the skin of his teeth. It is McCoy's relationship with Yvonne that saves him from himself. She gets a raw deal; her apparent suicide attempt jolts the book out of linguistic comedy, but we are never allowed to come too close to her. Then her anguish would have to be addressed, and this would be a different book. Until the penultimate chapter, Yvonne believes that McCoy is dead, but it is his reality we are led to address, not hers. She remains his satellite and his saviour, a depressingly familiar role for woman, and in the few chapters in which we switch to her point of view, language and insight are curiously sparse.

So it is the crisis of the alienated male which sustains the novel. McCoy remains the outsider, attempting to sell spyholes to the outside world to the citizens of Edinburgh, who, unlike him, have homes, sometimes even one another.

More often than not the I-could've-been-anyone line prompted people to look him up and down, conclude that he was anyone and shut the door in haste.

An uncomfortable book to read indoors in Edinburgh, costing nearly £9 more than a spyhole to the outcast world fitted by McCoy, but perhaps that much more illuminating.

Margaret Elphinstone

BOG, CLART & THAT SINKING FEELING

Towards the End, Joseph Mills; *The Shoe*, Gordon Legge; *Oiney Hoy*, Freddy Anderson; *The Trick is to Keep Breathing*, Janice Galloway; all Polygon, £7.95

The Concise Oxford Dictionary describes a novel thus: 'Fictitious prose narrative of volume length portraying characters and actions representative of real life in continuous plot'. None of the above really fulfil that remit. Why should they? Surely a novel can be whatever you want it to be? The formal arguments could run and run, but why is reviewing new Scottish novels like walking over a frozen bog? Perhaps because you realise that the world is hotting up and the ice is melting. That sinking feeling takes over: clart is more or less what you are going to experience. As our little country limps towards the 21st century are we ever going to get out of this infernal bog? Two of the above novels are bog, Two are not. Neither are they ice, thank goodness.

Joseph Mills' *Towards the End* is a puzzle. Polygon, it has to be said, have made a sturdy job of producing this book because it stood up well to the many times I flung it across the room. If the COD is any guide then this book plummets down beneath the moss. The "story" is non-existent: it follows a young lad leaving home, discovering his sexuality, falling in love with one of the colleagues at the bank where he works and mooning about Glasgow's gay clubs and pubs. Wow! Not that the reader doesn't want to feel sympathy for the main character, "I", "Me", or whoever it is, but the leaden prose and the attitudinal cringe of all that goes on stops any sympathy dead in its tracks. Begod, we are all Liberals here, are we not? As a series of events this book does not hang together. The characters rise like toxic whales struggling for air in a sea of pollution only to plunge again into the depths of mundanity. The author seems not really know what to do with people. The reader wanders around this book like a deranged Bedouin in search of an oasis. Unfortunately this novel is a mirage. Joseph Mills must learn (and here I preach) to take writing seriously, otherwise no reader can be expected to take him seriously. We do not need bad novels about the gay scene in Glasgow or anywhere else.

Gordon Legge, on the other hand, hasn't written a bad novel. He hasn't written a "novel" at all. Nothing much happens. There is a fight, granted. People do drink, I know this. They go to sleep. They get up. They play records. And they talk about all that. Incessantly and at length. And about football. This is a "youth" novel, set in some mythical Grangemouth/Falkirk of the mind that reminds me of an Instamatic photo: cheap, ingenious, and amazing for a minute if you like surfaces. Perhaps Legge is portaying the smallness of peoples' lives? Fair enough, but where is art? Absent. James Joyce did a brilliant fresco on a similar theme: we call it *Ulysses*. One fears this writer has slept with the NME for too long. Most of us know that the central belt is one long series of coal bings with grass growing on them. We need a story about the hopes, experiences and fears of the people who live among these bings. There are glimpses in "The Shoe", but they are all too brief and never followed up. Where oh where has the ambition in our novelists gone?

Well, I think I found it in *The Trick is to Keep Breathing* by Janice Galloway, and *Oiney Hoy* by Freddy Anderson. As the first two novels were conservative in range and style these two take risks and go places, yet, have strong vestiges of tradition behind them. It is the tradition of the poem rather than the novel and idiosyncratic poetic forms at that. Galloway employs the interior monologue with excursions in remembered dialogue, championed at its best by Shelley and Byron. Anderson, however, is pure ballad. His tale is both comic and epic, and a joy to read. In the story of young Oiney Hoy, Anderson gives us his vision of Ireland with all its contradictions and strengths. Its slightly predictability is offset against the ease with which the story is told. Nothing gets in the way of the narrative. Each hilarious scene and image, and there are many, which Anderson conjures is there for effect. This is story-telling of a high degree. The writer wants you to take this joke seriously; the reader would be foolish not to do so. In *Oiney Hoy* there is a kind of lunatic truth that springs from the Celtic gift for wit. Freddy Anderson asks you to question what you laugh at. We laugh. We question. We are further on in the world. Ireland is closer at hand.

Janice Galloway's *The Trick is to Keep Breathing* has a good story to it too. A young woman goes on holiday with her lover. He jumps into the swimming pool and bangs his head off the bottom. Dead. She then has a breakdown. The book is a chronicle of how that happens and what it is like for her. We are taken deep into the central character, can almost see her brain flipping over like some great machine. The prose is strong and vivid. Where it has to be sparse it is sparse. Where it has to be dense it is dense. But I found this a bleak book. The character's house is bleak. The people she meets are bleak. It's like reading the diary of Franz Kafka's little sister (if he had one). But one sees a fine writing talent here. The reader can follow the protagonist on her journey quite easily, despite the aforesaid bleakness. Yet, contradicting myself, I didn't find it an easy book to read. The mixture of gallows humour and psychological wrestling is a difficult broth to sup: at times it was just too grim. But once I'd finished the book I felt I knew something I did not know before. Quite what I'm not sure - "something" about loss and fear and grief, which is both.

The Trick is to Keep Breathing is a brave book. With Oiney Hoy it shares ambition, and a fine imagination. If, ultimately, they fail as novels it is because they have made a brave stab at achievement. Both these writers will keep writing. Their gifts and ambition will ensure that. As for Gordon Legge and Joseph Mills, I hope they keep writing too, for the novel needs constant stretching and re-inventing. I have a sneaking suspicion the COD is wrong. Who'd be a bloody novelist anyway?

George Gunn

PASTICHE OR PARODY?

The Quincunx, Charles Palliser, Penguin Books, £7.99; Linmill Stories, Robert McLellan, Canongate Classics, £4.95; A Thankful Heart, The Years Between, Kirsty, Callan B Cowan, Foreland Publishers, Bembridge, IOW, £8.99

This lengthy novel The Quincunx (1,200 pages) has received high praise in various reputable newspapers. The Times calls it a "brilliant pastiche of the mid-nineteenth-century novel", The Independent "an attempt to reproduce an Early Victorian novel". Apart from the confusion as to period, both agree that it tries to reproduce a style from the past, and inevitably comparison will be made with the greatest of the Victorian novelists, Charles Dickens. But Palliser is no Dickens. At times indeed one wonders if it is parody rather than pastiche. He sends his hero as a young boy to a Dotheboys Hall in the north of England after - yes - a long journey on the top of a stagecoach. Quigg's school far outdoes Mr Squeers' Dotheboys Hall in brutality: the boys feed from a trough full of potatoes and one is beaten to death. And here surfaces one of the differences in creativity between Palliser and Dickens - Squeers, grotesque, brutal, ugly is at the same time disgusting and comic and credible.

One of Dickens' gifts is the ability to make his characters, however odd, however bizarre, credible. Charles Palliser's villains - and they greatly outnumber the "goodies" - never seem real; they have no qualities but falsity, treachery and self-interest. The good characters, among whom are John Huffam the hero, and his mother, reveal a naivete not to say stupidity which makes it difficult for the reader to sympathise with them in their afflictions. For afflicted they are; because of the existence of a will (or is it two wills?) and a codicil thereto, John and his mother are harried from one place to another, each dwelling meaner

and more wretched than the one before but always in a low, dirty area of London. John's mother dies, leaving in a notebook an account of the complicated events which led to the making of the will and codicil. John Huffam, alone in the world, goes through an extraordinary series of adventures, including being almost murdered by drowning in a sewer, but eventually emerges as the sole remaining heir to the estate in question.

The complications of will and codicil are merely pegs on which hangs the extraordinary farrago of escapes, journeys, murders. The cast of characters is so large that an alphabetical list of them has been provided. But they are lifeless pieces in a nightmare game of multiple chess. Apart from the thieves and thugs whose speech is peppered with thieves' slang they all speak in the same stilted manner. One must, however, give credit for a fertile imagination in the creation of incidents strung along the thread of the plot. The description of low life in Victorian London is lively and even convincing, though the endlessly grim and grimy settings tend to a monotony of background. The problem of prostitution in Victorian London is treated coyly. How the hero-narrator was ever begotten is something of a mystery - his mother's wedding night was so interrupted by false quarrels, real murder, dashings back and forth to London by post-chaise. Perhaps the "several pages" she tore from the notebook on her death-bed and insisted on her son burning told of her seduction. The hero finally meets his father in a madhouse.

It is a witches' brew of a book; as if into a cauldron had been tossed a handful of Nicholas Nickleby, a measure of the Old Curiosity Shop, a pinch of Barnaby Rudge, a shake of Bleak House, and a sprinkling from Wilkie Collins for piquancy. It is not a question of plagiarism, but of flavour and parallelism. But the rapid succession of escapes and hurried journeys, the multifarious encounters of character with character do give the book verve and momentum.

Those who have already encountered the Linmill Stories will be delighted to find them gathered in a new collected edition. To write successfully about childhood is not easy. Either unreal idealisation takes over - as with Dickens' Little Nell and Paul Dombey - or the equally unreal depiction of children as brutal little savages. Lewis Carroll's Alice avoids sentimentality by her solemn reactions to preposterous situations, her endearing curiosity, and her practical common sense. It is easier to write of adolescence because it looms larger in the writer's experience; but few can remember with truthfulness and precision what being a child was really like. Robert McLellan had the gift, and this, combined with the setting - a fruit farm in the Upper Ward of Lanark in the days before mechanised farming - results in a work of immense appeal.

But there is much more to the stories than the charm of a boy's life and the setting in a vanished world. The tales give the impression of artlessness but are in fact most skilfully crafted. In 'The Robin', where Rab catches a robin which is then killed by a cat, the tension is carefully and subtly built up, and this is true of most of the tales. The characterisation is equally skilful. The small boy Rab with a tender conscience, always eager to know, hating to be done down or appear ridiculous, is splendidly depicted. One of the most touching tales tells how the young Rab has his baby curls cut, gets his first pair of trousers and discovers that this step to manhood is not the splendid thing he hoped for.

The other characters are equally well drawn - cousin Jockie, the grandfather, the grandmother are real rounded people, but always seen through the child's eyes. This is indeed the art which conceals art. Nor are the harsher aspects of the period and place glossed over. The hard seasonal work of harvesting the fruit was done by migrant Irish labourers, known collectively as "The Donegals"; and the permanent workforce consisted of boarded-out subnormal men; and Rab learns of the harsh realities of country life when his hand is caught in a trap set for rabbits. The language is a clear, unforced, natural Scots admirably suited to the themes, and playing a crucial role in building up the reality and atmosphere of the period in which the stories are set. One is overhearing rather than reading them. All these elements, narration, characters, language, combine to produce a Scots classic. It has its urban parallel in the neglected "Wee Macgreegor" but outsoars it in the consistent and unfaltering use of Scots. A book to treasure.

The three books by Callan B Cowan are to be followed by a fourth; the whole work to be known as A Tapestry of Faith. Volume 1 tells how Janet Chisholm in the 1880s brings up a family after the death of her husband in a train disaster on the day she was giving birth to a son Dugald. The Years Between and Kirsty recount the life of Janet's granddaughter, who has an unhappy childhood with a mother who dislikes her and a father who beats her from the highest motives. She trains as a nurse and at the end she is running a successful old folks' home, having survived the deaths of the two men she loved, attempted rape (hetero and lesbian) a bigamous marriage, and brutalisation by her (bigamous) husband; all this narrated in a curiously flat style, and flavoured with a simplistic pietism reminiscent of old-fashioned Sunday school prizes.   - Janet Caird

NEW POETRY

Robert Crawford, A Scottish Assembly, Chatto Poetry, £5.99; Graeme Fulton, Humouring the Iron Bar Man, Polygon, £6.95; Valerie Gillies, The Chanter's Tune, Canongate, £7.95; Donald Goodbrand Saunders, Findrinny, Dog and Bone, £4.50

The power of Valerie Gillies' The Chanter's Tune, is incantatory. Some poems were w.itten to be performed with the clarsach, and a musical element is deep in its movement. There are three sections: long sequences, shorter lyrics and translations. The translations, from Dante, 19th century Italian, and 17th century Gaelic, show the clarity of her work - her 'Lament for a Blind Harper' is refreshingly harsh as well as lyrical. The long sequences are more disappointing. 'The Hawkshaw Head', seven poems based on a Roman head carved in marble discovered near Tweedsmuir, successfully pivots on themes of past and present, though the whole is not as satisfyingly stark and enigmatic as its last stanza: "He has got his knowledge of the world already/ and from the high end of the valley/ two ravens fly near/ to speak into his ears." The end of 'The Mugdrum Sequence' has a battering rhythm and Gillies skilfully swings from this into two final stanzas, haunting after the original primativism. The short lyrics are more often captivating, like 'Three Voices', short pieces each attempting to uncover the rhythmic structures in everyday spoken syntax, lending a classic grandeur to a wittily vulgar and drunken late-night encounter at a party:

At a late-night party watched by no-one
who had not been drinking,
in sofas like groves
filled with leaves and birdsong,
. . . my hand grew beautiful
on his shoulder
and shrivelled to bone
when I took it away.

Often the end of poems hits the mark, rounding off something apparently disparate; this is evident in the sequences, and in lyrics like 'The Man in the Moss', 'The Ericstane Brooch', and the fine poem 'The Old Woman's Reel'. 'Spelt Wheat' is a spell in its incantation; 'Young Harper' is opaque and suggestive of legend, incantatory and distant, in a poetry whose language is concrete, insistently relevant. 'Quair Water' and 'Shepherd's Calendar' remind us of the dangers we face with "no natural balance left", when "everything shows the signs of a miasma,/ a time when the wrong people are ruling us". So the farmer, intimate with the land, becomes the artist in 'William Johnstone, Farmer and Artist', "cult animals and wonder beasts" roam the farm, and these legendary animals are easily part of the field's rhythm in her celebration of the union of earth and art.

The poems of *Findrinny* by Donald Saunders are light-hearted; sometimes slight, marginal jottings promising more. At best this is avoided, the language engagingly picked clean: "Grey frosts the fern/ and the mountain ash/ bears no memory of berries/ but a crackle is underfoot/ and a bird still/ flickers where the leaves were." ('Autumn') The book promises the lyrical but often stops at a poetry of punchlines, good-humoured and enjoyable, in the mischief of a poem like 'Putting the Clock Back', suggesting a few good ways of using the extra hour we're granted at the end of summer, "a tiny clawback/ from the dark season,/ for condemned summer/ an hour's reprieve". But the good-humoured voice turns into one-liners, sometimes witty, sometimes too pat, and this belies the poet's eye for a frostier imagery. Which is a shame; when the poetry refrains from taking the easy way out it's at its clearest, as in 'Inland Gull', which imagines the gull flying over rooftops, the "stiff waves of the city", or in the strong final sounds and images of 'Trawler', "crowned top-heavily with a squalling nimbus" of its own gulls, returning from fishing:

midnight discovers her a furtive poacher
engines chugging distantly,
                    close up to the shore.
The sound comes to me over still bays
in the dark of my sleep, and I think of her
dragging a shining hoard from its deep hold.

His fine sense of metaphor can override cliche.

Graham Fulton is one of Polygon's young poets, and his talent is in how he makes the casual central. In 'Marathon', on the sidelines of the Glagow marathon we're left with the image of "people in wheelchairs waving/ and wanting to do it as well/ with nuns beside them/ outside gates of home". So, casually, 'Marathon' becomes a poem about something else. Like a Scottish Frank O'Connor Fulton's poetry threatens to be as disposable, as much litter as the stuff lying about on the streets he describes: the movement of his poetry reveals a process of painful, step-by-step communication. A poem like 'Humouring the Iron Bar Man' can let you realise someone else's broken and careful breathing pattern in a disconcerting situation. Internal rhyme unifies the fragmented state of some poems; some degenerate into fragmented adolescent angst, some merely brush at a surface. Sometimes Fulton poses, like a William Carlos Williams with a conscious chip on his shoulder, as here in 'Lover of Nature':

it was
beautiful
and it got in

my bedroom somehow
and I put a tumbler over it
and watched it wear itself out
until I fell asleep and
I tipped it out the
window into the
watering
can

This can be likeable, or wearing; when cynical it seems little more than adolescent. But Fulton has an eye for ordinariness, ugliness, grime and violence, in a poem like 'Merry Man in Mid Land' or 'Dignified End' making these persuasively our cultural absolutes; he finds something seductive in talking about dogshit and heart attacks. His poetry can be cynical cliche, but can also sit right on the edge of calamity, working on several levels, as the subtle 'Eggs' does, set safely in its kitchen but really somewhere else entirely, skinning the thin surface of cruelty and ignorance.

In Robert Crawford's *A Scottish Assembly* there are rarities to be found: a poet of subtlety and intellect, uniting clarity and intelligence, a collection that's a challenge and a pleasure. Many poems are sharply funny. Crawford understands the generosity that comes from punning, in the sharp but affectionate 'The Only Emperor', homage to the Italian ice cream parlour and family. To him Scotland is a 'chip of a nation' where grandeur comes in cans; "We/ Sweep past their bungalows, heading back for the mainland./ They drive slowly to their prayer-meetings, different./ They watch us on their television." 'Bhidio', quoted above, apes a relation to translated poetry; Crawford is acutely aware of context. The core of his poetry is often a single sparking concept, static, out of which the poem expands.

His language is expertly placed. Scotland becomes 'The Land o' Cakes' where Highlanders 'were cleared like a table/ To make way for shortbread', eaten away leaving nothing but substitute. It's the place of "the unthinkable hills", where "intimate grasses blur with August rain", a country to inspire love poems as unexpectedly erotic as the texture of 'Tweeds', ("When dawn comes people will say they've heard/ Birdsong rise from our clothing").

A Scottish Assembly will persuade a sceptic that locality is enlightening. Poems like 'Souvenir of Scunthorpe' and 'Rep' counter loss of individuality; refuse to deny the individual voice, and the refreshing consciousness of self in his poems is constantly in balance with a necessary anonymity, like the self slipping out "quietly/ By the cellar door", off to sit privately in the garden in the poem called 'Robert Crawford'. This is the pluralism and the individuality of a major talent; poetry of a very satisfying calibre.- Alison Smith

CONTROVERSIALITIES

Roger Levy, *Scottish Nationalism at the Cross-roads*, Scottish Academic Press, £8.75; S. Henderson & A. Mackay, *Grit and Diamonds*, Stramullion, £5.95; Stuart Hood, *Garret O'Leary, Questions of Broadcasting*, Methuen, £14.99

Any new book on a Scottish topic is welcome. Relevant material, for the interested general public and for those trying to stimulate Scottish studies in educational institutions, is thin on the ground. Two recent books, *Scottish Nationalism at the Crossroads* and *Grit and Diamonds* come into this category. A third book, *Questions of Broadcasting*, although co-authored by a Scot, exemplifies an inexcusable metropolitanism.

Levy's study of the SNP has useful attributes but is disappointing overall. Although ostensibly covering both the seventies and eighties, it is about the SNP's development in the earlier period with a hasty and confused review of the 80s. No-one who did not already know the background to the SNP's response to the Constitutional Convention would find much enlightenment in the coverage given. By failing to appreciate the development of a new exclusiveness and drive for polarisation in the late 80s, he misses the link with earlier strands of fundamentalism.

We must, therefore, regard this as principally a study of the 70s and judge it on that basis. There is a useful discussion of the position of the SNP in the context of the wider political science debate on the classification of political parties and party systems and a chronological account of events which will be of use to students. But a major fault is the failure to place developments in the SNP's fortunes more clearly in the context of broader political and economic developments. Parties seldom have the opportunity to 'make' their own fortunes, certainly not over a longer period. They operate in a changing economic climate. They have to contend with other parties and groups whose strategies may change and whose performance outside Scotland may alter. These external factors have to be given a substantial place in the analysis of the developments in any new party.

The early 70s saw economic recession which weakened confidence in the capacity of Westminster to offer successful economic management. The February '74 election was fought against the background of the miners' strike and economic crisis, again discrediting existing political structures. The pick-up in Labour's fortunes after the mid-70s was linked to a period of comparative economic improvement. The referendum in '79 cannot be understood unless it is placed in the context of the 'winter of discontent', a period of unpopularity for the Labour government and an upturn of support for the Conservatives. The political and economic situation in March '89 was very different from that in the autumn of '88.

This is not the only explanation for developments. The mood of 1974, for example, was not that of negative protest but the atmosphere of genuine political idealism and enthusiasm. The SNP had developed skilful and imaginative political campaigning and captured a central part of the political agenda and the climate of disillusion with Westminster government and the other parties enabled the SNP strategy to bear fruit. Later the tactics of other parties and the change in economic conditions made it difficult to maintain that success irrespective of what choices the SNP made about policies and style. Labour acted both positively and negatively to counter SNP challenge. Positively, they offered a Scottish Assembly and the establishment of the Scottish Development Agency, and strengthened regional policy. Negatively, they, and the other parties, used all their considerable channels to discredit the SNP and put it on the defensive.

Levy's thesis that the SNP was substantially damaged by its failure to take a clear and consistent pro-devolution stance is very questionable. I strongly supported the party taking such a position because that was realistic and there was much to be said for a gradualist approach. But I could not say with conviction that a clearer and less-qualified support for the Scotland Bill would have altered the SNP's fortunes. For many of the electorate, political parties are not seen as objects of faith or tradition but as vehicles for change. What matters is the public's perception of who is best able to deliver change. This depends not on one factor but on a configuration of circumstances. In seeking vehicles for change, the electorate may have got priorities right; causes are more important than parties. This may be a bitter pill for party activists to swallow but if there is one lesson history should have taught us, it is that those who are instrumental in initiating change may not be those who ultimately achieve it. Levy's study will have uses for those with an academic interest in nationalist policies but it lacks the broader sociological perspective needed to provide real insight into the politics of the 70s and 80s.

If the literature on political nationalism is modest in extent, the literature on Scottish women is even sparser. *Grit and Diamonds* is a source book of women's campaigning activities in the 80s. So much of women's history has disappeared, ignored by those who recorded and analysed the events of their day. Women were and continue to be under-represented in the formal institutions of our society. The less formalised areas of social life where most female activity is concentrated are generally unrecorded, except by the novelist. The result reinforces the popular perception of women's activities as unimportant and marginal. As the editors comment, "unless women write down and record what happened yesterday, there will be nothing to be found even by those with the will to find it."

This is not an attempt to represent the experiences of the majority of women but to represent the experience of women working for social change. The editors did not seek to define in advance the areas of campaigning activity they wished to include. They wrote to local and national newspapers and magazines and contacted a wide range of campaigning groups. The result was 74 contributions. Some cover predictable areas of activity like local authority women's committees, trade unions, the peace movement, women's aid. But the range is refreshingly broad, from the Edinburgh Chinese Women's Group to the National Childbirth Trust, the campaign against sex shops in Aberdeen to women in the Glasgow Forum on Disability, Edinburgh Women in Media to expanding women's opportunities in manual trades. Most of the contributions although different in style share a personalised view which feels like women writing. They tend to be apologetic and not over-confident. A male equivalent, I suspect, would read very differently.

Questions of Broadcasting is co-authored by a Scot, Stuart Hood, but it displays a blinkered metropolitan perspective. It started as a project to compile an archive of interviews with key decision-makers in British television and a selection of these interviews have been used as the basis of the book. Garret O'Leary who conducted the interviews does apologise for the omission of any decision-makers outside London on the grounds that time and resources were limited. Given that the fieldwork took place over eleven months, this sounds more like a failure of interest rather than shortage of time. Scotland merits three casual passing references in the book. This criticism is not just another case of Scottish whingeing. Any book which does not take the trouble to make even a gesture towards the view outwith London, is simply being negligent.

The first section is a history of developments in British TV which covers familiar ground but may be of use to readers fresh to the subject. The main part looks at changes in the 80s - the role of the independents, cable and satellite, the Broadcasting Standards Council, the new contractual system for ITV. The views of leading figures in the industry and advertising focus differing responses to change. Within its limitations the book is a readable journalistic exercise. - Isobel Lindsay

PROTEST IN SCOTLAND

Covenant, Charter and Party, T Brotherstone (Ed), £16.50; *Fit for Heroes?* L Leneman, £17.50, both Aberdeen University Press; *The Crofters' War*, I M M MacPhail, Acair, £15.00.

The tradition of protest, if such it be, has absorbed a large share of modern Scottish historiography. It is perhaps just a matter of fashion. Elsewhere, eminent historians stopped studying the rulers of countries and turned instead to the ruled, in particular to those who for one reason or another rebelled against their rulers, with the result that major and memorable works were produced. As usual, lesser talents tagged along, mechanically applying the same techniques to confirm (never, I think, to deny) that there were indeed on their own patch protests organised by protesters.

Scotland might actually have made a good case-study of the opposite, of the relative absence of protest. Let us take a simple comparison, of how many people died for their political beliefs in the great age of revolutions, 1789-1848. In France, Germany, Italy, Austria, Hungary, Poland, indeed as close to home as Ireland, their numbers must have run into many thousands. Even in England there were probably some hundreds. I am open to correction, but so far as I can compute there were in Scotland 23, and this is on a very generous definition of dying for political beliefs: one mobster was shot dead in 1792, one radical was hanged in 1794, a dozen people met their deaths in the Militia Riot at Tranent in 1797, three more radicals were executed in 1820 and a handful of Chartists were accidentally killed in 1848. Since then, while in many other countries the political slaughter has gone on apace, nobody at all in Scotland has died for his or her beliefs.

This is not necessarily to assert that Scots have been obedient and conformist, but to point out that their protests have been held well within constitutional bounds. One might here make a useful distinction between that and actual revolt, which seeks to break such bounds. Unfortunately, it is not a distinction made by Terry Brotherstone who, as editor of a book sub-titled *Traditions of Revolt and Protest in Modern Scottish History*, just lumps wildly different movements together.

It leads him into a mess. The connecting thread he purports to discover turns out to be very tenuous indeed. It is that later protesters often made reference to the Covenanters in their rhetoric. Is this of any significance? After all, the same protesters were just as likely to refer to Wallace and Bruce, Mary Queen of Scots, Bonnie Prince Charlie, Uncle Tom Cobbleigh and all. So, we are solemnly taken back to the 17th century to see what we can dig up. Brotherstone's introduction wonders about the true nature of the Covenanters and whether - from a point of view undeclared but plainly Marxist - they were progressive or primitive: the "advanced guard of the common folk" or "men who are prepared to defy the stars in their courses". He asks if it is "possible to begin to uncover a tradition of subversive ideology (or even forms of struggle) drawing on the covenanting past and giving its meaning a new content in battles against new enemies?" I translate that as a strangulated call to start making history up so that we can use it in the politics of today - an urge to which other Scottish historians are not immune. I would be surprised, however, to see Brother Brotherstone in the vanguard when the Revolution comes. He is not even prepared to decode his own language.

Perhaps this pussy-footing is all to the good, for the first essay in the book, by Roger Mason, shows that the original Covenanters of the 1630s were drawn partly from feudal noblemen and clerical ideologues, not on the face of it having much to do with the popular fanaticism in the second phase of the movement, the Killing Time. The chain of continuity having been almost immediately broken, it is hard to see what remained of a tradition to be picked up by radicals of the 1790s, a matter ably examined by John Brims. He points out that they felt obliged to ban discussion of religion in their meetings. To a more perceptive symposiast than Brotherstone, this might have suggested an interesting paradox, that Scots' indifferentism in politics has often gone hand in hand with uncontrollable enthusiasm in religion. If he was seeking truly serious revolt against the constitution of the state, he might have looked to the Disruption, half a century later. It may not have been bloody or proletarian enough for the editor's taste, but it was one occasion when hundreds of thousands of Scots repudiated the authority set over them.

After such links as exist between the Covenanters and the Chartists or the Labour Party have been inconsequentially established, Brotherstone appears at the end to muddy the waters thoroughly. In a final essay, he attempts to bring out "a tradition of Marxist internationalism in recent British history", which he believes to have been represented by John Maclean. One has no reason to doubt that Maclean was a Marxist and that he found some working-class support, but this does not amount to a tradition. A tradition needs predecessors and successors. Where are they? To say that the Covenanters had anything to do with Marxist internationalism is simply to void words of their meaning. As for successors, perhaps Brother Brotherstone intends to lead us to the

barricades himself? Somehow I do not think so.

A second type of revolt he contrives to ignore altogether is that in the Highlands, one episode of which is covered in I M M MacPhail's book. He says "The Crofters' War is a comparatively modern name for the social unrest and political agitation which prevailed in the Highlands and Islands a century ago." It seems to me a bad name. War implies a minimum of scientific direction of massed forces, and the crofters never got anywhere near that: there are myths enough in Scottish history without our gratuitously manufacturing new ones. And to apply the label of 'war' to a sequence of events so inchoate is a little silly.

That said, this is still an admirably full and vivid account of the Highland troubles during the 1880s. MacPhail has skilfully exploited his local connections and mastery of Gaelic, as well as uncovering new sources. The depth of perspective he is thus able to add to the background does indeed allow us to appreciate why similar protests broke out in so many scattered places at once, and why the authorities were so alarmed.

A further wave of protest came after the First World War. This led to some redistribution of land in the North, and reinforced the policy of encouraging agricultural smallholdings in Scotland already introduced before 1914. Leah Leneman goes thoroughly into the administration of it and the difficulties it encountered, but here the wider background is a little too shadowy. Land reform had been an intermittent issue in Scottish politics since the beginning of the nineteenth century. We still lack an adequate study of it, and Dr Leneman could have rendered us a greater service by sketching the philosophical and political bases of what appears nowadays as a slightly dotty enthusiasm. She herself obviously regards land settlement as a Good Thing, and she might usefully return to the subject in future.

Michael Fry

THEATRE ROUND-UP

The remainder of Scotland views with massive indifference the supposed rivalry between Edinburgh and Glasgow, which is of concern only to the most parochial and mind-shrivelled in either city: the facts being that any fair and genuine comparison between the two - of the way they are run, for example, or of respective attitudes to the performing arts - would in neither case reveal extensive grounds for self-congratulation.

It was inevitable, once Glasgow had gathered up the onerously-expensive mantle of European City of Culture, brushing aside an inept and faint-hearted bid from Edinburgh in the process, that self-proclaimed cultural triumphalists of east and west should embark on a prolonged bout of trumpet practice. Attempting to assess whether an established three-week festival in one place has been more 'successful' than a one-off, twelve-month rolling programme of events in the other strikes me as an exercise roughly as fatuous as making a detailed personality-study of our new prime minister. An unjaundiced look at the experience of both cities might elicit one or two reflections - particularly as regards foreign-language drama - which might be useful to future organisers of theatrical jamborees.

First then, some disappointments. One of the severest was the wretchedly low ticket sales for Glasgow's season of international theatre, despite the participation of five highly-renowned foreign companies - including ones such as the Maly Theatre, which had previously made successful visits over here. On the other hand, the productions were all of undoubted quality, and the season did lend some real credibility to the Year of Culture's drama component.

Several of the Festival's imports also did poorly at the box office, though usually because they weren't much good. Amongst those were a couple of rum Japanese offerings (one of them, Half Gods, positively adolescent in its presentation of giant plugholes, Universes for the Disappearing Down of): also the Indian Kathkali version of King Lear. Of the latter it may be remarked that the mere fact of something's being incredibly old and amazingly traditional is not in itself a guarantee of interest; moreover, the knowledge that it had taken the cast five hours to get made up made those who did go to it feel guilty as well as bored.

Another Edinburgh disappointment was provided by what I am unhesitatingly prepared to accept was one of the greatest performers at the Festival. In Japan, Yukio Yoshimura has a long-since-earned and unassailable reputation as the finest living exponent of classical Noh-Kabuki dance. Briefly described, his 20-minute solo act consisted of a very elderly person emerging, very gradually, from a small cubicle, uplifting (exceedingly slowly) a nearby blossom, and then retreating, molto adagio, back into the cubicle.

Though plainly meticulous and extraordinary art, this intensely-studied work was, I fear, for inexperienced Western eyes and ears, more than a little daunting. I suspect that an appreciation of Noh-Kabuki is not easily to be picked up, a matter of mugging up on the conventions or blinking at a few instructive videos. I fancy, rather, that it takes the Japanese themselves a few years to acquire an informed understanding of this intricately-stylised form: and it is not everything that

can be instantly repackaged for consumption in an alien culture. (Yoshimura's dance comprised the first section of a double-bill brought over by Ninegawa; there was no avoiding the rare, ravishing fascination and startling beauty of the Mishima Yukio play which followed. Sotoba Komachi was one of the Festival's outstanding triumphs.)

Patience. However falteringly, I am gradually meandering towards what might be called a Nub, or even a Gist. Before that, however, I still require to explain what was disappointing about the visit of Korea's national company. In many ways, the Korean double production was exactly the sort of thing that an international festival should have; not least because, Korea having had one or two unfun times in the course of this century, the affirmation of national traditions and identity is considered a matter of some importance. Both of the Korean 'dance-drama' (Ch'unh Yang and Madame Tomi) had strong charms of exotic unfamiliarity: despite the Confucian underpinning, their common theme of faithfulness in love was one to find ready western acceptance; episodic structure allowed easy understanding of the storylines: choreography, design and music were all excellent, if not superlative; and the execution was, in general flawless.

So, was it not a shame that this unusual and stimulating theatrical experience, running in the middle of the Festival and for a few nights merely, should draw only moderate houses? It certainly is disappointing, but it ought not to be surprising. Theatre-goers operate on limited budgets, and if on holiday their time too may be limited. They are looking to enjoy themselves, to be thrilled, to be riveted; and putting my hand on my heart (that peculiarly vital organ of every theatre critic), had someone asked my opinion on whether to go to see the Koreans, or either of the splendid Branagh Shakespeares, or again the marvellously vivacious Hedda Gabler from New Zealand, I should have had to say: "If you go to the former, you will enjoy yourself, and your mind will be broadened. But I think you will get more out any of the latter." And in a comparable situation in Glasgow, I imagine I should have recommended the Citizens' resplendent Dumas, or their robust, vivid Jane Shore above any of the offerings from abroad.

To be honest, it is exceedingly rarely that a foreign-language production, especially when it is a non-European language, can hope to attain high popular success. The brilliant example is Ninegawa's Macbeth of a few Festivals ago: though of course, its strength was such that people who hadn't read Macbeth since schooldays suddenly found themselves able to remember every line.

I am taking it as near-axiomatic that bringing

over foreign drama is good in itself, so how best to go about it? When talking about the Koreans drawing "moderate" houses, I could equally well have used the terms such as "adequate", "very respectable" or even "as good as you are ever likely to get". For the fact is, I suggest, that the combination of Frank Dunlop and Edinburgh is about as optimal as it is possible to get.

Why? Well, consider first the adventitious advantages enjoyed by Dunlop. Large numbers of professional theatre people come up to Edinburgh for the Festival and the Fringe, and not just to perform (or to look for performers); seeing what's new and what's different is often their most important reason for coming, and these people form a substantial component of the audience for the more challenging work.

Having a well-established festival concentrated into three weeks helps, of course. But where Dunlop has been rather astute, in my opinion, has been in his policy of bringing over a significant variety of productions and giving them all fairly short runs. The greater choice sweeps up a larger number of what might be termed the special-interest groups: people who are studying the language or have some connection with the country. Ethnic interest is very noticeable, for example, at Polish, Jewish or Indian productions.

The accountants among you may be puzzled at one thing; since it is expensive to fly a large company half-way around the globe and back again, is it not more cost-effective for them to have a long run? Strangely enough, not necessarily. The economics of theatres are a congeries of imponderables. Suppose a company costs £5,000 a night if it attracts 100% audiences, but £15,000 a night if it brings in only 50%. Given that there must be a small maximum potential audience, is it more sensible to have it for a week or for a month, particularly if, as can happen, sponsorship or grant is available for the travelling costs?

On to less tensely cerebral matters. Communicado is one of our strongest and most innovative young companies, who this year have appeared in both Glasgow and Edinburgh, with *Jock Tamson's Bairns* and *Danton's Death* respectively. In both, the company's artistic standards were as immaculate as ever. (True, the *Danton* was criticised, I suppose with some justification, for insufficiently stressing the role of the populace; but I have no wild objection to seeing, for example, a performance as massively dominating and thrilling as that of Robert Carr as the eponymous hero.) Is there anyone, I wonder, who would disagree with the verdict that the second production offered more in the way of hard, virile theatre than the first, and by a generous margin? Or that the difference might have something to do with the relative merits of the respective playwrights?

This is not an entirely snide point: if there is one great lesson from the Year of Culture, it is this. By all means give out commissions to playwrights; please, let them have *lots* of commissions. But please, also, do not make the well-intentioned but quixotic and otiose mistake of asking a playwright to produce a play intended to "celebrate" something, particularly if the object of celebration happens to be "a way of life", "the rich tapestry of our past" or something along these lines.

The *worst* thing along these lines - full of false sentimentality, unredeemed by any inkling of solid purpose or honest feeling, may have been *The Ship* by Bill Bryden, who appears to have declined into a mere media man these days. That is not something you could ever say about Vaclav Havel, three short plays by whom - fine, well-crafted, utterly modern plays - were very successfully given a short exposure by an ad hoc Glasgow group, after a lot of scrambling about for a very modest sum of money.

Lastly for 1990, two prolonged rounds of applause, a wooden spoon, and a small regret. The applause is firstly to Musselburgh's Brunton Theatre for, in glorious defiance of all constrictions of space and budget, putting on a scintillating production of Shaw's *St Joan* which, had it been on in either city, would have held its own against anything Edinburgh or Glasgow had to offer all year. Thunderous cheers, too, for the Traverse's beautiful and haunting production of a contemporary Russian play, Gelman's *The Bench*; exquisite, compassionate writing was done full justice by production and direction.

The wooden spoon is for Theatre Workshop, partly to stir their sesame-seed and acorn-husk curry with: advanced multiculturalism, anti-able-bodiedism (that neologism, I promise you, actually exists) and environmental consciousness-raising have increasingly become recognised as crucial to any children's Christmas show, but with *Rasho, Champion of the Romanies* the workshop have gone further, incorporating ponderous fragments of a sociology lecture into their Yuletide drama. This certainly deserves recognition, and I assure you that the spoon has been fashioned from organically-grown wood.

And the small regret? Simply that - inertia, notoriously, being the major driving force in my life - I did not manage to make it to Perth for the premiere of *Gang Doon Wi' A Sang*, which for all I know might have proved the most brilliant play of the year if not the century. It was written by a certain Joy Hendry, whom I confidently expect to see appearing on the Melvyn Bragg show (or even Wogan) any day now.

Alasdair Simpson

PAMPHLETEER

As always Pamphleteer embraces a substantial and wide-ranging body of work. A B Jackson's *Snippets from the Powder Room* (from Maggie's Drum Press, 9 Great King Street, Edinburgh, £2) is one of the shortest of the books here, at 18 poems, but it is also in the handful I enjoyed most. The ideas can be complex and ambitious, his style at once elaborate and clean. From the direct ironic impact of his poem 'Kindergarten' to the impressionistic sweep of '40 Days' there is little to disappoint here, no excess baggage.

The same cannot be said for R L Cook's *The Daylight Lingers* (from the Lomond Press, 4 Whitecraigs, Kinneswood, Kinross, £3). The poems here can seem curiously old-fashioned, with odd echoes of Donne struggling for a rhyme. The poems are preoccupied with death, mortality, transience and loneliness, sometimes densely structured with ungainly syntactic convolution serving no particular end. Cook's work is at its best at its simplest, as in his use of haiku:

> The leaves on the street
> Scuttle like small crabs - crisp, gold
> In the Autumn wind.

His poem 'Rising Before Dawn On A Winter Morning To Make Coffee (from the Chinese)' is quite a mouthful as titles go, but the poem is unadorned and works simply and clearly.

Love Fables by Leeala (11 Learmonth Gardens, Edinburgh, £1) shows an idiosyncratic turn of humour, sometimes lapsing into the whimsical. Nonetheless, the poems are peppered with sharp images and insights into human relationships:

> When she had the last word
> He chopped up her tongue as a tasty
> hors d'oeuvre.
> Then he drank her breast dry
> And froze her love fruit.

Chameleons, cows and pussycats too populate these pages and, if sometimes a little trite, the best and barbed bits more than justify the modest cover price.

David Russell's *Nothing Hero* (from 8 McGregor Road, London, £1.50) is rather less appealing. The "epic" title-poem concerns the lives of Bill and Sarah. It is set in relentlessly rhyming couplets, a decision resulting in some tortuous constructions. Although not without its surprises much of the work attacks modern society and values, neither an original nor difficult target. Russell does not seem to like the world very much, which is fair enough, but he makes a pretty dreich and cluttered poetry of it.

Strangers and Pilgrims by Dorothy Brett Young (from Taxus at Stride, 37 Portland Street, Exeter, £4.99) describes itself as "religious (although not overtly so)", the religious content though *is* overt and, for a faithless old sinner like myself, both wearying and strident after a while. Still, after the bleak pessimism of Russell's work her faith seemed oddly appealing:

> As the year turns
> and we are purged of all our certainties,
> give us not answers.
> But the question, Lord.

This is from a sequence I enjoyed, 'In the Months that Follow'. Elsewhere her use of landscape is finely gauged and defined while sharp flashes and images ("teeth dry as ice") surface through the weave and give the proceedings a welcome boost.

Laurna Robertson's *The Ranselman's Tale* (Shetland Publishing Company, 4 Midgarth Crescent, Lerwick, £2.50) centres on the wreck of El Gran Grifon, flagship of the Spanish Armada, on Fair Isle in 1588. The tale in itself is fascinating as Robertson spans out to explore the relationship, sometimes only barely sustained, between the 300-odd seamen and the sparse, and sparsely-provided, population of only 17 families. Although the verse can be too low-key, Robertson can produce an eerie aura to her work, simply, in the citation of islanders' names below: "Magnus and I took leave of them and gathered/ at Briggs/ The householders: Vaasetter, Pund,/ Stonibreck,/ Taing, Shirva, Sculties, Tait, Leogh,/ Gaila, Quoy,/ Hool, Kennaby, Stackhool, Mires and Busta./ We told them of the galleon,/ and the shipwrecked men/ That we must harbour in our homes."

Christina S Tait's *Spindrift* (from Hjogaland, Trondra, Scalloway, Shetland, hbk £8.95) also focusses on Shetland, both past and present. The poetry is stylistically unadventurous, often marred by tired and predictable rhyme:

> Poor Planet Earth - we use you
> Like a whore for our careless pleasure
> We pour corruption into your veins,
> Defile you beyond measure.

Prevalent concerns are destruction, debasement of the landscape, the stupidity of mankind, celebration of the natural world and the (presumed) innocent, clean world of children. All very worthy and largely true, endearing enough but never startling, challenging or original. She celebrates plain talk and direct expression, which she practices, but the effect is to render her work one-dimensional, to rob it of depth and surprise.

To wind up, two exceptional collections, (both from Lines Review Editions, MacDonald Publishers, Edgefield Road, Loanhead). James Greene's *A Sad Paradise* (£6.95) is an often densely-textured yet vivid collection, never failing to jolt your expectations. There are surrealistic edges here with impressive freshness. From the heart which becomes "a collapsed accordion" to these perspctive-warping lines from 'Minster Lovell':

In the manor, a stone's throw away, a girl
Playing hide-and-seek with her young man
Pulled the lid of a chest over her oval head
And vanished, though her skeleton was found -
Today the real players are in the wings
                              like ghosts.

There is a bizarre colouring to Greene's view of the world and even at his most direct, in a poem like 'The Stag', his work retains an other-worldliness that is very welcome. His deeply unsettling 'Letter from Eton' stands out in this carefully structured collection, but all of the work here will reward and sustain the closest reading.

Angus Martin's The Larch Plantation (£4.95) is focussed on rough and ragged landscape, the roughness of life and death on the land and sea. As in Andrew Jackson's work there is no dead wood here, with Martin displaying a fine sense of rhythm and rhyme, often ironically counter-pointing his subject matter:

His father stirred him,
old Duncan, squat and muscular,
smelling of tar and fish,
and for thirty years obdurate
at the helm of his own skiff,
his pride as bright to the end
as superlative yacht varnish.
His hand, as hard as barnacles,

There are sometimes echoes of MacCaig here, "A rock dislodged by a foraging goat /falls out of place and tries its weight in air", but only echoes: Martin's work is very much his own and there is much here that shines. His aunt, her "body frail as an old stuffed heron", or, in 'Lamb', where he writes of walking "straight into horror", the animal still living but beyond help, the eyes "half stabbed from his head". The poem concludes:

and the hoodies and black-backit gulls
will have his eyes
and steaming entrails,
and what remains
a fox by night will drag away.

If Martin's settings and themes are consistently of the harsh world he inhabits they are never tired or tedious and there's a wry, cold wit behind the poems that never fails to produce a shudder. In 'Dykes' he writes, "nothing understands a dyke like a weasel", adding a few lines later, "Birds rear their delicate families in dykes,/ and weasels certainly know that too". The Larch Plantation is a powerful first collection, highly recommended.

Thom Nairn

CATALOGUE

Titanic is the still-in-process Collected Letters of Thomas and Jane Welsh Carlyle (Duke UP), Vol 16 Jan-July 1843, Vol 17 Aug '43-Mar '44, Vol 18 April-Dec '44+index, $39.95/ £35.65 per vol, prefaced with a charming mix of detail, domestic and otherwise: "March: JWC pleased to find that Mazzini, Darwin and Elizabeth Pepoli do not like Jewsbury; TC attends Chas. Lyell's lectures on geology; finishes Past and Present; visits the Chinese exhibition; hears Wellington speak in the House of Lords; complains about the neighbours' piano playing; Jewsbury finally leaves." Carlyle wrote letters for 37 years more: so there's a long way yet. This huge and worthy project is a labour of love, carried out with impeccable scholarship.

Its blurb trumpets "the crowning achievement of Scottish chronicle-writing, the most substantial work of literature produced in Scotland in the Middle Ages", Scottichronicon was composed in Latin by Walter Bower, abbot of Inchcolm in the 1440s; no version in English has been attempted till now. Aberdeen UP's parallel text annotated edition is necessary and thorough (Vol 2, Books III & IV are just out, ed. John and Winifred MacQueen, £25.00 per vol; vol 9 emerged in 1987). But the translation should someday come out alone: Merlin, Lailoken, Malcolm et al. There is a lively disquisition on the nature of the traitor; legend; moralising; observation. Charlemagne's son Louis the Pious dies, a girl in the territory of Toul abstains three years from food and drink, in a Gaul hailstorm a block of ice falls, six by fifteen by two feet. Modern literature is so narrow!

Scottish Studies 9 (Peter Lang, DM 105), Silvia Mergenthal's James Hogg: Selbstbild und Bild, is an admirably thorough study of that writer - necessary reading for all students of that writer. European interest in Scottish writing grows apace.

Reprints include George MacDonald, The Princess & the Goblin/The Princess & Curdie (OUP pbk. £4.95), James Leslie Mitchell's Spartacus Scottish Academic Press, Scottish Classics 14), £6.75, his Grey Granite (£3.50) now a Canongate Classic alongside Magnus Merriman, (satiric romp, 1930s Scots Renaissance setting, Hugh Skene = HMacD, etc.) by Eric Linklater, The End of an Old Song, J.D. Scott, Fergus Lamont by Robin Jenkins, Dance of the Apprentices, disgracefully out of print for years, by Glasgow's Edward Gaitens (all £4.95), The Corn King and the Spring Queen, Naomi Mitchison (£6.95), who provides her own new introduction to that book; others have variously useful new prefaces by other hands. The same house's The Adventures of Endill Swift by Stuart McDonald, comic fantasy "originally for children" (£8.95) is OK but its "appeal to adults" misses this one. New Kelpies are *Quest for a Maid*, Frances Mary Hendry (£2.75), witchcraft &c. 13th C.; *Murdo's War*, Alan Temperley (£2.95) well-written thriller, 1943; *Pictures in the Cave*, George Mackay Brown, reprint from 1977 (£2.50); Pamela Cockerill's *Donkey Rescue*, for slightly younger weans (£2.25). Mainstream redo Wm. McIlvanney's *A Gift from Nessus* (£4.95) and Brian McCabe's *The Lipstick Circus* (£5.95). Neil Gunn's *Highland Pack*, splendid 1939 collection of prose on Highland scenes/themes, is a handsome hardback from Richard Drew (£12.95). Tom Nairn's *The Enchanted Glass* is now a Picador (£5.99).

Acair (7 James St. Stornoway) have in *Togail Tir/Marking Time* ed. Finlay MacLeod (£12.95) a remarkable picture of various ways of seeing Highland, mainly Outer Isle, landscape. Some amazing old maps, a real curiosity. Central and consistently good value are the books in John Donald's *Discovering* series, £7.50 each: *Argyll, Mull & Iona* with Willie Orr's solid text, *Speyside*, Francis Thompson, *Arran*, Alastair Gemmell, *Angus & the Mearns* I.A.N. Henderson, whose pages on Grassic Gibbon are strong. This no merely for-tourist-use series but serious and lively. Highly commended. Plusher, pitched a shade lower is Craig Mair's *Stirling - The Royal Burgh* (J Donald £13.95). Comparisons between old and new photographs make Alastair Durie's *Vanishing Edinburgh* (Keith Murray Publications, £12.95, more striking than Hamish Coghill's *Edinburgh - The Old Town* (John Donald £9.95) fine though much there is. *Edinburgh Past & Present*, by Maurice Lindsay/David Bruce (Robt. Hale £12.95) is a bumper bag of elements in the other two, half & half text & photos. But THREE such new books? Is therr no ithers aaready?

Makars' Walk (Scottish Poetry Liby £6.95) is a fair hantle o Embro Auld Toun poetry, ed. Duncan Glen, with his memoir of strolls and striking unhackneyed choices of b&w prints. Big format, £14.95 from Canongate (with John Cooper's modern foties) Ann MacSween's *Skye*, a book about the island; and Robbie Jack/Owen Dudley Edwards' *The Edinburgh Festival* with its many snaps. Canongate's *Glasgow Girls* (£30.00) is stunning, Glasgow 1880-1920 with special emphasis on "women in art and design" ed. Jude Burkhauser: not at all predictable, in an every sense brilliantly designed big book; "Words by Christopher Rush" says the front of their *Where the Clock Stands Still - The East Neuk of Fife*: Ferms, fishers, Fife touns, fine foties onywey (£10.95). At £9.95 Mainstream show *Paintings from the Clydesdale Bank Collection*, well done catalogue/anthology of Scottish art 19/20th Cent. Alas Joseph McKenzie's *Gorbals Children*

(Richard Drew £11.95) has many photos overbig for what's there (like much modern Scots painting). Joanna Blythman's *Eating Out in Edinburgh & Glasgow*, £3.95 Canongate, is full of the kind of advice it's a pleasure to take. Blythman knows what she's talking about - and she can write well too. Wilma Paterson's *Lord Byron's Relish* (Dog & Bone, £7) is a celebration of that writer's love of comestibles, but it's also a typographical salmagundi which will make your eyes cross. Aberdeen UP's *Scottish Museums & Galleries* calls itself *The Guide* (£4.95). Better use that than stay in with *The State of the Language* (£17.50, Faber) ed. Christopher Ricks & Leonard Michaels. There is a bizarre unificationist tendency at work: what the Devil is THE language and who the WE who speak it? Poems, a bit of a novel, David Dabydeen 'On Not Being Milton . . .' 530 pages of more and less interesting essay, pretentious tosh, Roger Scrotum's study of G--fr-y -rch-r's 'fiction'. I suppose people *ought* to be interested?

Whitfur nae Ivor Cutler rerr? Intriguing artist subtle shuffler of mannerisms, with Martin Honeysett as illustrator. £6.99 gets *Glasgow Dreamer* (Methuen) their latest, and miles different from Ralph Glasser's *Gorbals Boy at Oxford* (Pan, £4.99) a book of intelligence with pungently ironic title: son of Jewish immigrants and bracingly with a bit of iron in him. Miles away again from these Scots/Jewish memoirists is David Daiches' *Was, a Pastime from Time Past* (Richard Drew, £4.99), profuse and learned and in its play with words, memories, learning: a most appealing book.

Some anthologies of poetry: especially commended is *Hinterland, Caribbean Poetry from the West Indies & Britain* ed. E.A. Markham (Bloodaxe £7.95). The major figures are decently represented, no mere token selections, and with introductions this is a smart purchase for anyone wishing to find out about poets like Berry, D'Aguiar, Nichols, Kwesi Johnson, Walcott . . . Prodigious. Less so but intriguing is Bloodaxe's *high on the walls* (£5.95) with new unpublished poems by MacCaig, Cutler and others who have read at Newcastle's Morden Tower, a famous venue over decades now. *The Chatto Book of Love Poetry* (ed. John Fuller, £13.99) presents a series of texts without initial indication as to authorship (you look them up at the end). The choice is laudably enterprising. Margaret Elphinstone's *A Treasury of Garden Verse* (Canongate £14.95) seems pricey, but has a decent introduction and intriguing later choices. *A Roomful of Birds* (Collins £12.95) is the 1990 annual anthology of Scottish short stories. I suspect none of the authors in this book was known in the genre ten years back. Some are quite famous now. But perhaps that proves nothing whatever.

NOTES ON CONTRIBUTORS

Chris Bendon, winner of the Scottish Open Poetry Competition in '88-'89, he also writes criticism, short fiction and plays. He lives in Wales.

Janet Caird: novelist and poet, born in Malawi, now living in Inverness.

Fergus Chadwick: b.1946, Surrey-based poet, poetry tutor, painter, book-keeper.

Margaret Elphinstone lectures in English at Strathclyde. Has published gardening books, two novels and a book of short stories (out soon).

George Faludy, b.1910, maybe Hungary's greatest living poet, recently returned after 3 decades of self-imposed exile.

Michael Fry: writer, broadcaster, historian, and prominent Scottish Tory.

Sam Gilliland: Writer, broadcaster b. Ayrshire 1939. Co-organiser, Scottish Open Poetry Competition. Published in UK, India, Spain & USA.

Alasdair Gray, according to *Unlikely Stories* (Canongate, 1983): educated and became ... residing and remaining ... and intending ... then on became in ... and again and later again ... He still is and resides ... and intends and hopes ... and may ... but is certain to one day.

George Gunn, playwright and poet, a native of Caithness. Recently completed a radio play, *Piper at the Gates*. His latest collection of poetry, *Sting* published soon in Chapman New Writers Series.

Anne Hay: Born Perth, now lives in Edinburgh, working in Polygon's Original Prints department & on BBC Radio.

Peter Hughes: translator & teacher living in Rome.

Fred Johnston: poet and critic born Belfast, based in Galway. Extensively published. Initiated Cuirt, Galway's Poetry Festival, in 1986.

Isobel Lindsay, prominent in SNP and Scottish Constitutional Convention, lecturer in Sociology Department of Strathclyde University, Glasgow.

Ann Lingard: research scientist & university lecturer, now freelance writer.

Thom Nairn is Managing editor of Cencrastus, poet, critic and teacher.

Hugh McMillan, b.1955 in Dumfries, teaches Dumfries Academy. Published in many languages; first major book, *Tramontana* published by Dog & Bone.

Donny O'Rourke: arts producer at STV, Glasgow.

Thomas Orszag-Land, b.Hungary 1938, Poet, journalist, translator, foreign correspondent. *Berlin Proposal* published last year by Envoi Poets' Press.

Michael O'Siadhail edits *Poetry Ireland Review*, on the Arts Council of Eire and the Advisory Committee on Cultural Affairs. Most recent collection of poetry, *The Chosen Garden* was recently published by the Dedalus Press.

Dorothy Porter/McMillan lectures in English Lit. at Glasgow University, is on Glasgow Herald's team of theatre critics. Editor of critical editions.

Alasdair Simpson, theatre critic of Times Scottish Education Supplement.

Alison Smith: playwright, poet and critic, currently teaching at the Department of English Studies, Strathclyde University.

Raymond Vettese lives Montrose and teaches US base, Edzell. First Soutar Creative Writing Fellow in Perth, Preses of the Scots Language Society.

Christopher Whyte, poet and critic, lectures Scottish Literature department of Glasgow University, having previously taught English in Rome.